Berlitz® Audio Aids

S0-BDS-027

Just listen and repeat!

60 minute cassettes teach you basic expressions with the right accent before you depart. 32 page script included, with pronunciation and complete text.

	Cassettes Quantity	LP Records Quantity	8-Track Quantity
Arabic	218		
Danish	200	225	
Dutch	212	237	
Finnish	201	226	
French	202	227	802
German	203	228	803
Greek	204	229	
Hebrew	205	230	805
Italian	206	231	806
Japanese	207	232	
Norwegian	208	233	
Portuguese	214	239	
Russian	209	234	809
Serbo-Croatian	215		
Spanish (Castil)	210	235	810
Spanish (Lat Am)	213	238	813
Swedish	211	236	

English for Visitors	Cassettes	LP BRIT	LP USA
For French	250	830	246
For German	260	835	247
For Italian	280		248
For Spanish*	290		249
For Danish	300	850	
For Dutch	270	855	
For Finnish	310	860	
For Norwegian	320	870	
For Swedish	330		
For Japanese	Cas. BRIT 340	Cas. USA 345	
* also available as 8-Track	890		

Total Units _____

Please count the total number of units requested and complete the reverse side of this order form.

11403

$	£
From New Jersey	**From London**
Total units _____	Total units _____
at $7.95 each	at £4.95
Total amount enclosed	Total amount enclosed
$ _____	£ _____
(N.J. residents add	(VAT is included)
sales tax)	

Name _____

_____

Address _____

_____

_____

Please complete and return this order form to:

Traveller's
Shopping Service   or
600 Grand Avenue
Ridgefield, NJ 07657
USA

Traveller's
Shopping Service
8, Trident Way
Brent Road
Southall
Middlesex UB2 5LS
England

Please order Berlitz books through your bookseller. Should you encounter any difficulties, write directly to any of the distributors listed on the back cover.

BERLITZ®

TURKISH
FOR TRAVELLERS

By the staff of Editions Berlitz

Library of Congress Catalog Card Number: 73-20998

4th printing 1982

Printed in Switzerland

Editions Berlitz
1, avenue des Jordils
1000 Lausanne 6, Switzerland

Preface

You're about to visit Turkey. Our aim is to give you a practical phrase book to help you on your trip.

Turkish for Travellers provides:

* all the phrases and supplementary vocabulary you'll need on your trip

* a wide variety of tourist and travel facts, tips and useful information

* a complete phonetic transcription, showing you the pronunciation of all the words and phrases listed

* special sections showing the replies your listener might give to you—just hand him the book and let him point at the appropriate phrase. This is especially practical in certain difficult situations (doctor, car mechanic, etc.) It makes direct, quick and sure communication possible

* a logical system of presentation so that you can find the right phrase for the immediate situation

* quick reference through colour coding. The major features of the contents are on the back cover; a complete index is given inside.

These are just a few of the practical advantages. In addition, the book will prove a valuable introduction to life in Turkey. There's a comprehensive section on Eating Out, giving translations and explanations for practically anything one might want. Trouble with the car? Turn to the mechanic's manual with its dual-language instructions. Feeling ill? Our medical section provides the most rapid communication possible between you and the doctor.

You'll often find phrases with three dots (...) and followed by a list of words. This means that you can make up the phrase of your own choice by replacing the dots with any of the words from that list. When there's no space between the dot and the following letter or letters—for example, ...*e*—it indicates that what follows the dots is a suffix.

To make the most of *Turkish for Travellers,* we suggest that you start with the "Guide to Pronunciation". Then go on to "Some Basic Expressions". This not only gives you a minimum vocabulary, it helps you to pronounce the language.

We are particularly grateful to Mr. Charles W. Applegate, Mr. Jak Barbut, Mr. Hakan Çöteli and Miss Sevil Müren for their help in the preparation of this book, and also to Dr T.J.A. Bennett who devised the phonetic transcription. We also wish to thank Turkish Airlines and the Turkish Tourism and Information Bureau for their assistance.

We shall be very pleased to receive any comments, criticisms and suggestions that you think may help us in preparing future editions.

Thank you. Have a good trip.

Throughout this book, the symbols illustrated here indicate small sections where phrases have been compiled that your foreign listener might like to say to *you*. If you don't understand him, give him the book and let him point to the phrase in his language. The English translation is just beside it.

Guide to pronunciation

This and the following chapter are intended to make you familiar with the phonetic transcription we have devised and to help you get used to the sounds of Turkish.

As a minimum vocabulary for your trip, we've selected a number of basic words and phrases under the title "Some Basic Expressions" (pages 11–16).

An outline of the spelling and sounds of Turkish

You'll find the pronunciation of the Turkish letters and sounds explained below, as well as the symbols we're using for them in the transcriptions. Note that Turkish has some diacritical letters—letters with special markings—which we don't have in English.

The imitated pronunciation should be read as if it were English except for any special rules set out below. It is based on Standard British pronunciation, though we have tried to take account of General American pronunciation also. Of course, the sounds of any two languages are never exactly the same; but if you follow carefully the indications supplied here you should be able to read our transcriptions in such a way as to make yourself understood.

Letters shown in bold print should be read with more stress (louder) than the others.

Consonants

Letter	Approximate pronunciation	Symbol	Example	
b, d, f, l, m, n, p, t, z	as in English			
c	like j in jam	j	**cep**	jehp

ç	like **ch** in **ch**ip	ch	**çocuk**	**cho**jook
d, n, t	as in English but with the tongue touching the upper teeth, not the gums behind them			
g	1) before or after **a, ı, o, u** as in **go**	g	**gam**	gahm
	2) before or after **e, i, ö, ü**, it is followed by a **y** sound as in angular	gʸ	**göz**	gʸurz
ğ	1) when at the end of a word or followed by a consonant it lengthens the preceding vowel		**dağ**	dar
	2) when preceded and followed by **a, ı, o, u,** the preceding vowel is lengthened, and the following vowel more or less disappears		**uğur**	oor
h	always pronounced as in **h**it, except in the name Mehmet where it is silent	hh	**mahkeme**	**mahh**kehmeh
j	like **s** in plea**s**ure	zh	**müjde**	mew**zh**deh
k	1) before or after **a, ı, o, u**, like **c** in **c**ool	k	**bakan**	**bah**kahn
	2) before or after **e, i, ö, ü**, it is followed by a **y** sound, like **c** in **c**ure	kʸ	**kürek**	kʸewrayk
r	with the tip of the tongue touching the gums just behind the teeth; it is always pronounced	r	**kar**	kahr
s	always as in **s**o, never as in i**s**	s/ss	**masa**	**mah**ssah
ş	like **sh** in **sh**ell	sh	**şimşek**	**sheem**shehk
v	often pronounced so weakly that it sounds more like a **w**	v	**yuva**	**yoo**vah

PRONUNCIATION

y	1) when at the beginning of a word or after a consonant, like **y** in yes	y	**yağ**	yar
	2) when **y** comes between **e, i, ö,** or **ü** and a consonant, the vowel is lengthened		**öyle**	urleh
	3) when preceded by a vowel, it becomes part of a diphthong			

Vowels

In Turkish, vowels are generally short but can be lengthened by **ğ** or **y**; or when used in some words borrowed from Persian or Arabic.

a·	1) generally like the vowel in Northern English pronunciation of man	ah	**adam**	ahdahm
	2) when long, like **a** in father	ar*	**âdil**	ardeel
e	1) usually as in met	eh	**evet**	ehveht
	2) sometimes (especially when long) like **a** in English late; not a diphthong	ay	**teyze**	tayzeh
ı	pronounced with the centre of the tongue high, the lips unrounded and the tip of the tongue behind the lower front teeth, alternatively, with your lips spread as if to say **ee**, try to say the vowel of put	ı	**karı**	kahrı
i	as in machine	ee	**iğne**	eeneh
o	like **o** in tone but without diphthong effect; sometimes like **o** in hot	o	**orada**	orahdah

* The **r** should not be pronounced when reading this transcription.

ö	like **ur** in f**ur** but with the lips a little rounded	ur*	**ömür**	**ur**mewr
u	1) generally like **u** in p**u**ll	oo	**uzak**	**oo**zahk
	2) in some words, especially those beginning with lu or nu, more like **oo** in l**oo**t	oo	**numara**	**noo**mahrah
ü	pronounce **ee** as in s**ee** but round your lips, without moving your tongue	ew	**üç**	**ew**ch

â, û, i, aa

1) The circumflex accent (ˆ) is written over **a** and **u** to show that the preceding **g, k** or **l** is followed by a short **y** sound, e.g., **Lâtin** (**lʸah**tin).

2) Elsewhere the circumflex indicates that a vowel is long and can also indicate the length after **g**, k or l, though not always.

3) To indicate long **a** after a **g**, k or l (not followed by a short **y** sound) **aa** is used, e.g., **kaatil** (**kar**til).

Diphthongs

ay	like **igh** in s**igh**t	igh	**ay**	igh
ey	like **ay** in s**ay**	ay	**bey**	bay
oy	like **oy** in c**oy**	oy	**koy**	koy

Doubled Consonants

These represent not two separate sounds, but a single, long one, like, for example, the **p-p** in lam**p-p**ost.

Glottal Stop

This is found in words borrowed from Arabic, but is tending to disappear from everyday speech.

Stress

Stress is variable and depends partly on the position of the word in the sentence and on the suffixes present. As a *very* general guideline, stress often falls on alternate syllables. Also, the voice rises slightly on the last syllable.

* The r should not be pronounced when reading this transcription.

Some basic expressions

Yes.	Evet.	ehveht
No.	Hayır.	hahyır
Please.	Lütfen.	lewtfehn
Thank you.	Teşekkür ederim.	tehshehkkʸewr ehdehreem
Thank you very much.	Çok teşekkür ederim.	chok tehshehkkʸewr ehdehreem
That's all right.	Birşey değil.	beershey dehgʸeel

Greetings

Hello.	Merhaba.	mehrhhahbah
Good morning.	Günaydın.	gewnighdın
Good afternoon.	Tünaydın.	tewnighdın
Good evening.	İyi akşamlar.	eeyee ahkshahmlahr
Good night.	İyi geceler.	eeyee gʸehjehlehr
Good-bye.	Allahaısmarladık.* Güle güle.**	ahllahhhahısmahrlahdık gʸewleh gʸewleh
See you later.	Sonra görüşürüz.	sonrah gʸurrewshewrewz
This is Mr...	... Bey.	... bay
This is Mrs...	... Hanım.	...hahnım
This is Miss...	... Hanım.	...hahnım
I'm very pleased to meet you.	Tanıştığımıza memnun oldum.	tahnıshtırmızah mehmnoon oldoom
How are you?	Nasılsınız?	nahssılsınız

* Said by the one who's leaving
** Said by the one who remains

Very well, thank you.	**Çok iyiyim, teşekkür ederim.**	chok **ee**yee**yeem** teh**shehk**-k^yewr eh**deh**reem
And you?	**Siz nasılsınız?**	seez **nah**ssılsınız
Fine.	**İyiyim.**	ee**yee**yeem
Excuse me.	**Affedersiniz.**	ahfeh**dehr**seeneez

Questions

Where?	**Nerede?**	**neh**rehdeh
Where's...?	**... nerededir?**	... **neh**rehdehdeer
Where are...?	**... neredeler?**	... **neh**rehdehlehr
When?	**Ne zaman?**	neh **zah**mahn
What?	**Ne?**	neh
How?	**Nasıl?**	**nah**ssıl
How much?	**Ne kadar?**	neh kah**dahr**
How many?	**Kaç tane?**	kahch **tah**neh
Who?	**Kim?**	keem
Why?	**Niçin?**	nee**cheen**
Which?	**Hangisi?**	hahng^y**ees**see
What do you call this?	**Bunun adı ne?**	**boo**noon ahdı neh
What do you call that?	**Şunun adı ne?**	**shoo**noon ahdı neh
What does this mean?	**Bu ne demektir?**	boo neh deh**mehk**^yteer
What does that mean?	**Şu ne demektir?**	shoo neh deh**mehk**^yteer

Do you speak...?

| Do you speak English? | **İngilizce biliyor musunuz?** | eeng^yee**leez**jeh bee**lee**eeyor **moos**soonooz |
| Do you speak German? | **Almanca biliyor musunuz?** | ahl**mahn**jah bee**lee**eeyor **moos**soonooz |

Do you speak French?	**Fransızca biliyor musunuz?**	frahnsızjah beeleeyor moossoonooz
Do you speak Spanish?	**İspanyolca biliyor musunuz?**	eespahnyoljah beeleeyor moossoonooz
Do you speak Italian?	**İtalyanca biliyor musunuz?**	eetahlyahnjah beeleeyor moossoonooz
Could you speak more slowly, please?	**Lütfen daha ağır konuşur musunuz?**	lewtfehn dahhah arır konooshoor moossoonooz
Please point to the phrase in the book.	**Lütfen cümleyi kitapta gösterin.**	lewtfehn jewmlehyee kᵛeetahptah gᵛurstehreen
Just a minute. I'll see if I can find it in this book.	**Bir dakika, bakayım kitapta var mı.**	beer dahkᵛeekah bahkahyım kᵛeetahptah vahr mı
I understand.	**Anlıyorum.**	ahnlıyoroom
I don't understand.	**Anlamıyorum.**	ahnlahmıyoroom

Can...?

Can I have...?	**... rica edebilir miyim?**	... reejah ehdehbeeleer meeyeem
Can we have...?	**... rica edebilir miyiz?**	... reejah ehdehbeeleer meeyeez
Can you show me...?	**Bana ... gösterebilir misiniz?**	bahnah ... gᵛurstehreh-beeleer meesseeneez
Can you tell me...?	**Bana ... söyleyebilir misiniz?**	bahnah ... surylehyeh-beeleer meesseeneez
Can you please help me?	**Lütfen bana yardım edebilir misiniz?**	lewtfehn bahnah yahrdım ehdehbeeleer meesseeneez

Wanting

I'd like...	**... istiyorum.**	... eesteeyoroom
We'd like...	**... istiyoruz.**	... eesteeyorooz
Please give me...	**Lütfen bana ... verin.**	lewtfehn bahnah ... vehreen

Please give it to me.	**Lütfen onu bana verin.**	lewtfehn onoo bahnah vehreen
Please bring me...	**Lütfen bana ... getirin.**	lewtfehn bahnah... gᵛehteereen
Please bring it to me.	**Lütfen onu bana getirin.**	lewtfehn onoo bahnah gᵛehteereen
I'm hungry.	**Acıktım.**	ahjıktım
I'm thirsty.	**Susadım.**	soossahdım
I'm tired.	**Yorgunum.**	yorgoonoom
I'm lost.	**Kayboldum.**	kighboldoom
It's important.	**Önemlidir.**	urnehmleedeer
It's urgent.	**Acveledir.**	ahjehlehdeer
Hurry up!	**Acele edin!**	ahjehleh ehdeen

It is/There is...

It's...	**O ... dur.**	o ... door
Is it...?	**O ... mudur?**	o ... moodoor
It isn't...	**O ... değildir.**	o ... deheeldeer
There's/There are...	**... vardır/... vardır.**	... vahrdır/... vahrdır
Is there/Are there...?	**... var mıdır/... var mıdır?**	... vahr mıdır/... vahr mıdır
There isn't/There aren't...	**... yoktur/... yoktur.**	... yoktoor/... yoktoor
There isn't any/There aren't any.	**Hiç yoktur/Hiç yoktur.**	hheech yoktoor/hheech yoktoor

A few common words

big/small	**büyük/küçük**	bewyewkᵛ/kᵛewchewkᵛ
quick/slow	**çabuk/yavaş**	chahbook/yahvahsh
early/late	**erken/geç**	ehrkᵛehn/gᵛehch
cheap/expensive	**ucuz/pahalı**	oojooz/pahhahlı

SOME BASIC EXPRESSIONS

near/far	**yakın/uzak**	yahkın/oozahk
hot/cold	**sıcak/soğuk**	sijahk/soook
full/empty	**dolu/boş**	doloo/bosh
easy/difficult	**kolay/güç**	koligh/gʸewch
heavy/light	**ağır/hafif**	arır/hhahfeef
open/shut	**açık/kapalı**	ahchık/kahpahlı
right/wrong	**doğru/yanlış**	dorroo/yahnlısh
old/new	**eski/yeni**	ehskʸee/yehnee
old/young	**ihtiyar/genç**	eehhteeyahr/gʸehnch
beautiful/ugly	**güzel/çirkin**	gʸewzehl/cheerkʸeen
good/bad	**iyi/kötü**	eeyee/kʸurtew
better/worse	**daha iyi/daha kötü**	dahhhah eeyee/dahhhah kʸurtew

A few prepositions and some more useful words

at	**...da/...de/...ta/...te**	...dah/...deh/...tah/...teh
on	**üstünde**	ewstewndeh
in	**içinde**	eecheendeh
to	**...a/...e**	...ah/...eh
from	**...dan/...den/...tan/...ten**	...dahn/...dehn/...tahn/tehn
inside	**içinde**	eecheendeh
outside	**dışında**	dıshındah
up	**yurakıda**	yookahrıdah
down	**aşağıda**	ahshardah
before	**önce**	urnjeh
after	**sonra**	sonrah
with	**ile**	eeleh
without	**...sız**	...sız
through	**arasında**	ahrahssındah

towards	...a doğru/ ...e doğru	...ah **dorroo**/...eh **dorroo**
until	...a kadar/ ...e kadar	...ah kah**dahr**/...eh kah**dahr**
during	**esnasında**	ehs**nahss**ındah
and	**ve**	veh
or	**veya**	veh**yah**
not	**değil**	de**reel**
nothing	**hiçbirşey**	**heech**beershay
none	**hiçbiri**	**heech**beeree
very	**çok**	chok
also	**da/de**	dah/deh
soon	**hemen**	**heh**mehn
perhaps	**belki**	**behlk**ʸee
here	**burada**	**boo**rahdah
there	**orada**	**o**rahdah
now	**şimdi**	**sheem**dee
then	**daha**	**dah**hah

A very basic grammar

Even though it now uses the Roman alphabet, the Turkish language still remains somewhat exotic, being completely different from our own language and, indeed, from any other European language. Its proven relations are a mere handful of central Asian dialects and Mongolian, though some experts believe it to be a member of a far-flung family of languages possibly including Finnish and Hungarian.

It's impossible to cover Turkish grammar completely in only a few pages so only its salient features will be dealt with here.

Two essential characteristics of Turkish, which pervade every aspect of the language, are its use of suffixes and its vocal harmony. We'll begin with these.

Suffixes

Where English uses separate words such as prepositions, possessive adjectives and verbs, Turkish expresses the sense by means of suffixes, i.e. endings added to the root word.

Some incredibly long words can be built up this way. An example with which the Turks themselves like to startle foreigners is this:

Avrupalılaştırılamıyanlardanmısınız?
Are you one of those who can't be Europeanized?

However, you'll be able to get by without having to master such dinosaur-like constructions!

For ease of comprehension we've often split up words into their component parts, though in normal writing no such breaks appear.

GRAMMAR

Vocal harmony

In any one word you can only use vowels from one of two distinct groups. The choice is set by the first vowel in the word.

Vowel group 1	Vowel group 2
a, ı, o, u	**e, i, ü, ö**

ad   name   **köy**   village
adı   his name   **köyü**   his village

As an exercise, look back at our dinosaur word given under *suffixes* and you'll find that, since the first vowel is **a,** *all* the subsequent vowels are also taken from Group 1. Foreign words often constitute exceptions to this rule.

Closely related to vocal harmony is a sort of consonantal change that operates in Turkish. The terminal consonant often changes when a suffix is added to the root word.

mutfak   kitchen   direct object: **mutfağı**

The rules for determining exactly which vowel from one of the two groups is inserted and which new consonant replaces the original terminal consonant are very complicated. A bit of astute detective work will sometimes be required before you realize that, for instance, the standard plural ending for nouns **-ler** can also come out as **-lar, -ler, -lör,** etc.

Nouns

As in English, the Turkish noun has no gender. However, there is no definite article (*the*) either.

The plural is formed by adding **-ler** to the singular (subject to the rules of vocal harmony).

çiçek   flower   **çiçekler**   flowers
araba   car   **arabalar**   cars

GRAMMAR

The English indefinite article (*a, an*) is expressed in Turkish by **bir.**

polis   the policeman   **bir polis**   a policeman

Turkish nouns have six cases, differentiated by suffixes. They are as follows: absolute (roughly the same as our subject), accusative (direct object), possessive (also used for noun complement), dative (indirect object), locative (indicating where something is) and ablative (indicating movement away from a person or a thing). The suffixes are subject to the rules of vocal harmony and consonantal change.

	Singular		Plural
Absolute	**köy**	the village	**köyler**
Accusative	**köyü**	(I see) the village	**köyleri**
Possessive	**köyün**	of the village	**köylerin**
Dative	**köye**	(I gave) to the village	**köylere**
Locative	**köyde**	in the village	**köylerde**
Ablative	**köyden**	from the village	**köylerden**

GRAMMAR

Adjectives

The adjective preceeds the noun and doesn't change.

uzun yol   the long road   **uzun yollar**   the long roads

Pronouns

	I	you	he/she/it	we	you	they
Absolute	**ben**	**sen**	**o**	**biz**	**siz**	**onlar**
Accusative	**beni**	**seni**	**onu**	**bizi**	**sizi**	**onları**
Possessive	**benim**	**senin**	**onun**	**bizim**	**sizin**	**onların**
Dative	**bana**	**sana**	**ona**	**bize**	**size**	**onlara**
Locative	**bende**	**sende**	**onda**	**bizde**	**sizde**	**onlarda**
Ablative	**benden**	**senden**	**ondan**	**bizden**	**sizden**	**onlardan**

The subject (absolute) pronoun is not generally used in a sentence since the verb ending is enough to indicate the person.

Possessive adjectives

The English possessive adjectives (*my, your*, etc.) are expressed in Turkish by suffixes (which again follow the rules of vocal harmony and consonantal change):

After a consonant				After a vowel			
my	-im	our	-imiz	my	-m	our	-miz
your	-in	your	-iniz	your	-n	your	-niz
his/her/its	-i	their	-leri	his/her/its	-si	their	-leri

köyüm my village **köyü** his village

Note that in this example the **-üm** and **-ü** endings are variants of the basic **-im** and **-i** endings, due to the rules of vocal harmony (see what we mean by detective work?).

Postpositions

A certain number of English prepositions are expressed in Turkish by postpositions (that is, words placed *after* the noun).

kardeş brother **kardeşi gibi** like a brother

Verbs

In Turkish the future, present and past tenses overlap to a certain extent, and the examples given below can in most cases be used to cover all these three tenses.

We're giving just two simple verbs here, *to be* and *to take*

The verb *to be* merely takes the form of a suffix.

I am	-im	we are	-iz
you are	-sin	you are	-siniz
he/she/it is	(-dir/-tir)	they are	(-dir/-tir)ler

Evde-y-im. I'm at home. (the **y** goes in to avoid the contact of two vowels)

The verb *to take:*

Infinitive: almak root element: **al** (+ **ı** to avoid the contact between two consonants)

I'm taking	**alı-yor-um**	we're taking	**alı-yor-uz**
you're taking	**alı-yor-sun**	you're taking	**alı-yor-sunuz**
he's taking	**alı-yor**	they're taking	**alı-yor-lar**

-yor indicates present tense. **-um, -sun,** etc., are harmony-modified versions of the verb *to be*.

Negative form

A verb is turned into the negative by inserting **-me** immediately after the root element of the verb.

beklemek to wait
bekli-yor-um I'm waiting   **bekle-mi-yor-um** I'm not waiting

Questions

The interrogative particle **mi** turns the immediately preceding word into a question.

Türksünüz. You are Turkish.
Türk müsünüz?* Are you Turkish?

* **mi** becomes **mü** due to vocal harmony.

Arrival

You've arrived. Whether you've come by ship or plane, you'll have to go through passport and customs formalities. (For car/border control, see page 145.)

There's certain to be somebody around who speaks English. That's why we're making this a brief section. What you really want is to be off to your hotel in the shortest possible time. And here are the steps to get these formalities out of the way quickly.

Passport control

Here's my passport.	**İşte pasaportum.**	eeshteh pahssahportoom
I'll be staying...	**... kalacağım.**	...kahlahjarım
a few days	**Birkaç gün**	beerkahch gʸewn
a week	**Bir hafta**	beer hhahftah
two weeks	**İki hafta**	eekee hhahftah
a month	**Bir ay**	beer ahy
I don't know yet.	**Henüz bilmiyorum.**	hhehnewz beelmeeyoroom
I'm here on holiday.	**Burada tatilde bulunuyorum.**	boorahdah tahteeldeh booloonooyoroom
I'm here on business.	**Burada iş için bulunuyorum.**	boorahdah eesh eecheen booloonooyoroom
I'm just passing through.	**Geçerken uğradım.**	gehchehrkehn oorahdım

If things become difficult:

I'm sorry, I don't understand.	**Özür dilerim, anlamıyorum.**	urzewr deelehreem ahnlahmıyoroom
Is there anyone here who speaks English?	**Burada ingilizce bilen biri var mı?**	boorahdah eengʸeeleezjeh beelehn beeree vahr mı

Customs

The chart below shows you what you can bring in duty free.*

Cigarettes	Cigars	Tobacco	Spirits (liquor)	Wine
200	or 50	or 200 grams	1	or 1
			(in opened bottles)	

After collecting your baggage, leave by the green exit if you have nothing to declare or by the red exit if you have goods on which you must pay duty. Spot checks are frequently made in the green channel.

Tape recorders, transistor radios and similar items should be registered in the traveller's passport to ensure free export. (For currency restrictions, see page 134.)

I've nothing to declare.	**Deklare edecek birşeyim yok.**	dehk^ylahreh ehdehjehk^y beershehyeem yok
I've a...	**... var.**	... vahr
carton of cigarettes	**Bir karton sigaram**	beer **kahr**ton seegah**rahm**
bottle of whisky	**Bir şişe viskim**	beer **shee**sheh **vees**k^yeem
bottle of wine	**Bir şişe şarabım**	beer **shee**sheh shah**rah**bım
Must I pay on this?	**Bunun gümrüğü var mı?**	boo**noon** g^yewm**rew**yew vahr mı
How much?	**Ne kadar?**	neh kah**dahr**
It's for my personal use.	**Şahsım içindir.**	**shahh**sım eecheen**deer**
It's not new.	**Yeni değildir.**	yeh**nee** dereel**deer**

* All allowances subject to change without notice and measurements approximate.

Pasaportunuz, lütfen.	Your passport, please.
Deklare edecek birşeyiniz var mı?	Do you have anything to declare?
Lütfen bu çantayı açın.	Please open this bag.
Bunun için gümrük ödemeniz lâzım.	You'll have to pay duty on this.
Başka bagajınız var mı?	Do you have any more luggage?

Baggage—Porters

The porter may take your bags through customs for you. He'll then wait till they've been cleared. Note the number on his badge.

Porter!	Hamal!	hhahmahl
Please take these bags.	Lütfen bu çantaları alın.	lewtfehn boo chantahlahrı ahlın
That's mine.	O benimkidir.	o behneemkeedeer
That ... one.	Şu...	shoo
big/small	büyüğü/küçüğü	bewyewyew/kᵞewchew-yew
blue/brown	mavisi/kahverengisi	mahveehssee/kahh-vehrehngeessee
black/plaid	siyahı/ekosesi	seeyahhı/ehkossehssee
There's one piece missing.	Bir parça eksik.	beer pahrchah ehkᵛsseekᵞ
Take these bags to the...	Bu çantaları ... götürün.	boo chahntahlahrı ... gurtewrewn
bus	otobüse	otobewsseh
collective taxi	dolmuşa	dolmooshah
luggage lockers	emanet kasasına	ehmahneht kahssahssınah
taxi	taksiye	tahkseeyeh
How much is that?	Ne kadar ödeyeceğim?	neh kahdahr urdehyehjehyeem

Note: The normal rate is 2.50–3.50 liras per bag. Have some small change ready.

Changing money

You'll find a bank at most airports. If it's closed, don't worry.
You'll be able to change money at your hotel. Full details
about money and currency exchange are given on pages
134–136.

Where's the nearest currency exchange?	**En yakın kambiyo bürosu nerededir?**	ehn yahkın kahmbeeyo bewrossoo nehrehdehdeer
Can you change these traveller's cheques (checks)?	**Bu seyahat çeklerini bozabilir misiniz?**	boo sehyahhaht chehkʸlehreenee bozahbeeleer meesseeneez
I want to change some...	**... bozdurmak istiyorum.**	... bozdoormahk eesteeyoroom
dollars	**Dolar**	dolahr
pounds	**Sterlin**	stehrleen
Can you change this into Turkish liras?	**Bunu türk lirasına çevirebilir misiniz?**	boonoo tewrk leerahssınah chehveerehbeeleer meesseeneez
What's the exchange rate?	**Resmî kur nedir?**	rehsmee koor nehdeer

Directions

How do I get to...?	**...e nasıl gidebilirim?**	...eh nahssıl geedehbeeleereem
Where's the bus into town?	**Şehire otobüs nereden kalkar?**	shehheereh otobewss nehrehdehn kahlkahr
Where can I get a taxi?	**Nerede bir taksi bulabilirim?**	nehrehdeh beer tahksee boolahbeeleereem
Where can I rent a car?	**Nereden bir otomobil kiralıyabilirim?**	nehrehdehn beer otomobeel keerahlıyahbeeleereem

Hotel reservations

Many terminals have a hotel reservation service or tourist
information office. You're sure to find someone there who
speaks English.

Car rental

A limited number of car hire firms operate in the major cities. Advance bookings are advisable to ensure having the vehicle of your choice.

It's very likely that someone at the agency will speak English. But if nobody does, try one of the following:

I'd like a...	... istiyorum.	... eesteeyoroom
car	**Bir otomobil**	beer otomo**beel**
large car	**Büyük bir otomobil**	bewyewk^r beer otomo**beel**
small car	**Küçük bir otomobil**	k^yewchewk^r beer otomo**beel**
sports car	**Bir spor otomobil**	beer **spor** otomo**beel**
I'd like it for...	... için istiyorum.	... eecheen eesteeyoroom
a day/four days	**Bir gün/Dört gün**	beer g^yewn/durt g^yewn
a week/two weeks	**Bir hafta/İki hafta**	beer hhahftah/eekee hhahftah
What's the charge per...	... kirası ne kadardır?	... keerahssı neh
day/week	**Günlük/Haftalık**	g^yewnlewk^y/hhahftahlık
Does that include mileage?	**Kilometre ücreti dahil mi?**	keelomehtreh ewjrehtee dahheel mee
What's the charge per kilometre?	**Kilometre başına ücret nedir?**	keelomehtreh bahshınah ewjreht nehdeer
Is petrol (gasoline) included?	**Benzin dahil midir?**	behnzeen dahheel meedeer
I want full insurance.	**Tam sigorta istiyorum.**	tahm seegortah eesteeyoroom
What's the deposit?	**Depozit ne kadardır?**	dehpozeet neh kahdahrdır
I've a credit card.	**Kredi kartım var.**	krehdee kahrtım vahr
Here's my driving licence.	**İşte şoför ehliyetim.**	eeshteh shofur ehhleeyehteem

Note: An international driving licence is often required (available through your home motoring association).

Taxi and dolmuş

Taxis can be hailed in the street. It's usually best to negotiate the fare before you get in. For some trips, e.g., airport to town there may be a fixed rate. (In Istanbul, taxi drivers are required to carry a printed card showing the official rates for sample destinations.)

There's also a type of shared taxi called a *dolmuş* to be found in Ankara, Istanbul and Izmir. Like the local bus, the *dolmuş* runs over a specific route, picking up and discharging passengers who all pay the same fare.

Where can I get a taxi?	**Nerede bir taksi bulabilirim?**	nehrehdeh beer **tahksee** boolahbeeleereem
Please get me a taxi.	**Bana bir taksi çağırın, lütfen.**	bahnah beer **tahksee** charrin **lewtfehn**
What's the fare to...?	**...e ücret ne kadardır?**	...eh ewjreht neh kahdahrdir
How far is it to...?	**Orası ...e ne kadar uzaktır?**	orahssı ...eh neh kahdahr oozahktır
Take me to...	**Beni ... götürün.**	behnee ... gᵛewtewrewn
this address	**bu adrese**	boo ahdrehsseh
the town centre	**şehir merkezine**	shehheer mehrkehzeeneh
the ... Hotel	**... Oteline**	... otehleeneh
Turn...at the next corner.	**Ilk köşebahşından ...a dönün.**	eelk kurshehbahshındahn ...ah durnewn
left/right	**sol/sağ**	sol/sar
Go straight ahead.	**Doğru devam edin.**	doroo dehvahm ehdeen
Please stop here.	**Burada durun, lütfen.**	boorahdah dooroon lewtfehn
I'm in a hurry.	**Acelem var.**	ahjehlehm vahr
Could you drive more slowly?	**Daha ağır kullanabilir misiniz?**	dahhah arır koollahnahbeeleer meesseeneez
Could you help me to carry my bags?	**Çantalarımı taşımama yardım eder misiniz?**	chahntahlahrımı tahshımahmah yahrdım ehdehr messeeneez

FOR TIPPING, see inside back-cover

ARRIVAL

Hotel—Other accommodation

The Turkish Ministry of Tourism and Information has rated some of the nation's hotels, motels and boarding houses. There are also a large number of establishments which, while not listed by the tourism ministry, are nevertheless checked by local authorities.

Otel
(otehl)

The government places hotels in five categories going from luxury to fourth class. Luxury and first-class hotels offer the maximum in comfort and facilities on a par with international standards. Other classes offer average to modest accommodation.

Motel
(motehl)

The tourism ministry places motels in three classes. After first and second class, there are motels which have an *M* rating but are equivalent to first or second class motels.

Pansiyon
(pahnseeyon)

Furnished flats (apartments) called *pansiyonlar* are available to let for short periods. They often have one or two bedrooms, a kitchenette and a bathroom. Such accommodation is found mostly in Istanbul and seaside resorts.

Turistik pansiyon
(tooreesteek
pahnseeyon)

Recognized but not rated by the tourism ministry, these boarding houses are usually private flats (apartments) which are partially used for lodging tourists. There's usually a salon and dining room for boarders. Again, such accommodation is generally found only in Istanbul and seaside spas. In summer, youth organizations like the National Turkish Student Union (Milli Türk Talebe Birliği) arrange lodging for students.

HOTEL

In this section, we're mainly concerned with the smaller and medium-priced hotels, motels, and boarding houses. You'll have no language difficulties in the luxury and first-class hotels where most of the staff speak English.

In the next few pages we consider your requirements—step by step—from arrival to departure. You needn't read through all of it; just turn to the situation that applies.

Checking in—Reception

My name is...	**Adım ...'dır.**	ahdım ...dır
I've a reservation.	**Rezervasyonum var.**	rehzehrvahsyonoom vahr
We've reserved two rooms, a single and a double.	**Biri tek, diğeri iki kişilik olmak üzere iki oda rezerve ettirdik.**	beeree tehk deeyehree eekee keesheeleek olmahk ewzehreh eekee odah rehzehrveh ehtteerdeek
I wrote to you last month.	**Size geçen ay yazmıştım.**	seezeh gehchehn ahy yahzmıshtım
Here's the confirmation.	**İşte konfirmasyon.**	eeshteh konfeermassyon
I'd like...	**... istiyorum.**	... eesteeyoroom
a single room	**Tek yataklı bir oda**	tehk yahtahklı beer odah
a double room	**Çift yataklı bir oda**	cheeft yahtahklı beer odah
two single rooms	**İki tek yataklı oda**	eekee tehk yahtahklı odah
a room with twin beds	**İki kişilik ayrı ayrı yataklı bir oda**	eekee keesheeleek ahyrı ahyrı yahtahklı beer odah
a room with a bath	**Banyolu bir oda**	bahnyoloo beer odah
a room with a shower	**Duşlu bir oda**	dooshloo beer odah
a room with a balcony	**Balkonlu bir oda**	bahlkonloo beer odah
a room with a view	**Manzaralı bir oda**	mahnzahrahlı beer odah
a suite	**Bir daire**	beer daheereh
We'd like a room...	**... bir oda istiyoruz.**	... beer odah eesteeyorooz
in the front	**Ön tarafta**	urn tahrahftah
at the back	**Arka tarafta**	ahrkah tahrahftah
facing the sea	**Denize bakan**	dehneezeh bahkahn
facing the courtyard	**Avluya bakan**	ahvlooyah bahkahn

It must be quiet.	**Sakin bir yer olsun.**	sah**keen** beer yehr olsoon
Is there...?	**... var mı?**	... vahr mı
air conditioning	**Soğuk hava tertibatı**	so**rook** hahvah 'tehrteebahtı
heating	**Kalorifer**	kahloreefehr
a radio in the room	**Odada radyo**	odah**dah** rahdyo
a television in the room	**Odada televizyon**	odah**dah** tehlehveezyon
laundry service	**Çamaşır servisi**	chahmah**shır** sehrveessee
room service	**Oda hizmeti**	odah heezmehtee
hot water	**Sıcak su**	sı**jahk** soo
running water	**Akarsu**	ahkahrsoo
a private toilet	**Dahilî tuvalet**	dah**heelee** toovahleht

How much?

What's the price...?	**... ücret ne kadardır?**	... ew**jreht** neh kahdahr**dır**
per week	**Bir haftalık**	beer **hahf**tahlık
per night	**Bir gecelik**	beer geh**jeh**leek
for bed and breakfast	**Yatak ve kahvaltı için**	yah**tahk** veh kahh**vahltı** ee**cheen**
excluding meals	**Öğünler hariç**	urewn**lehr** hahreech
for full board	**Tam pansiyon için**	tahm pahnseeyon ee**cheen**
for half board	**Yarım pansiyon için**	yah**rım** pahnseeyon ee**cheen**
Does that include...?	**Buna ... dahil mi?**	boonah ... dah**heel** mee
breakfast	**kahvaltı**	kahh**vahltı**
meals	**öğünler**	urewn**lehr**
service	**servis**	sehr**veess**
tax	**vergi**	vehrg^{y}ee
Is there any reduction for children?	**Çocuklar için indirim var mı?**	chojook**lahr** ee**cheen** een**deereem** vahr mı
Do you charge for the baby?	**Bebek için ücret alıyor musunuz?**	beh**behk** ee**cheen** ew**jreht** ah**lıyor** moossoonooz
That's too expensive.	**Çok pahalı.**	chok pah**hahlı**
Haven't you anything cheaper?	**Daha ucuz birşeyiniz yok mu?**	dah**hah** oo**jooz** beersheyee**neez** yok moo

How long?

We'll be staying...	...**kalacağız.**	... kahlah**jah**ız
overnight only	**Sadece bir gece**	sah**deh**jeh beer gᵛeh**jeh**
a few days	**Birkaç gün**	beer**kahch** gᵛewn
a week (at least)	**Bir hafta (en azından)**	beer **hahf**tah (**ehn** ahzındahn)
I don't know yet.	**Henüz bilmiyorum.**	heh**newz** beelmeeyoroom

Decision

May I see the room?	**Odayı görebilir miyim?**	o**dah**yı gureh**bee**leer **mee**yeem
No, I don't like it.	**Hayır, hoşuma gitmiyor.**	**hah**yır hoshoo**mah** gᵛeet**mee**yor
It's too...	**Çok ...**	chok
cold/hot	**soğuk/sıcak**	so**rook**/sı**jahk**
dark/small	**loş/küçük**	losh/kᵛew**chewk**
noisy	**gürültülü**	gᵛewrewl**tew**lew
I asked for a room with a bath.	**Banyola bir oda istemiştim.**	bahn**yoloo** beer odah eesteh**meesh**teem
Do you have anything...?	**... birşeyiniz var mı?**	... beersheh**yee**neez vahr mı
better/bigger	**Daha iyi/Daha büyük**	**dah**hah **ee**yee/**dah**hah bew**yewk**
cheaper/quieter	**Daha ucuz/Daha sakin**	**dah**hah oo**jooz**/**dah**hah sah**keen**
Do you have a room with a better view?	**Daha hoş manzaralı bir odanız var mı?**	**dah**hah hosh mahnzah**rah**lı beer odah**nız** vahr mı
That's fine. I'll take it.	**Gayet iyi, bunu tutuyorum.**	gah**yeht** **ee**yee boonoo tootoo**yo**room

Bills

These are usually paid weekly or upon departure if you stay less than a week. Some hotels offer a reduction of 50% for children under eight or nine.

HOTEL

Tipping

A service charge of 15 per cent is normally included in the bill, but you can ask:

| Is service included? | **Servis dahil mi?** | sehrveess dahheel mee |

Even if your room or meals are included as part of a package tour, you'll still want to remember the maid and the waiter.

Registration

Upon arrival at a hotel, motel or boarding house you'll be asked to fill in a registration form *(formüler)*. It asks your name, home address, passport number and next destination. It's almost certain to carry an English translation. If it doesn't, ask the desk-clerk *(resepsiyonist)*:

| What does this mean? | **Bu ne demektir?** | boo neh dehmehk**teer** |

The desk-clerk will probably ask you for your passport. He may want to keep it for a while, even overnight. Don't worry. You'll get it back. He may want to ask you the following questions:

Pasaportunuzu görebilir miyim?	May I see your passport?
Bu formüleri doldurur musunuz?	Would you mind filling in this registration form?
Lütfen burayı imzalayın.	Please sign here.
Ne kadar kalacaksınız?	How long will you be staying?

| What's my room number? | **Oda numaram kaç?** | odah noomah**rahm** kahch |
| Will you have our bags sent up? | **Çantalarımı yukarı gönderir misiniz?** | chahntahlah**rımı** yoo**kah**rı g'urndeh**reer** meesseeneez |

HOTEL

FOR TIPPING, see also inside back-cover

Service, please

bellboy	**belboy**	behlboy
maid	**famdöşambr**	fahmdurshahmbr
manager	**müdür**	mewdewr
room service	**oda hizmetçisi**	odah heezmehtcheessee
	(vale)	(vahleh)
switchboard operator	**santral**	sahntrahl
waiter	**garson**	gahrson

In Turkish, you don't use a title like waiter, sir or miss to get
the attention of a hotel staff member for service. But you
should preface your request with the polite expression, *Lütfen
bakar mısınız* (**lewt**fehn bah**kahr mıssınız**), which means
"Would you please serve us?"

Please ask the maid to come up.	**Lütfen famdöşambra yukarı çıkmasını söyleyiniz.**	lewtfehn fahmdurshambrah yookahrı chıkmahssını surlehyeeneez
Who is it?	**Kim o?**	keem o
Just a minute.	**Bir dakika.**	beer dahkeekah
Come in!	**Girin!**	gveereen
The door's open.	**Kapı açık.**	kahpı ahchık
Is there a bath on this floor?	**Bu katta banyo var mı?**	boo kahttah bahnyo vahr mı
How does this shower work?	**Bu dus nasıl çalışır?**	boo doosh nahssıl chahlıshır
Where's the plug for the shaver?	**Traş makinası için priz nerededir?**	trahsh mahkeenahssı eecheen preez nehrehdehdeer
What's the voltage here?	**Burada voltaj nedir?**	boorahdah voltahj nehdeer
Can we have breakfast in our room?	**Sabah kahvaltısını odamızda alabilir miyiz?**	sahbahh kahhvahltıssını odahmızdah ahlahbeeleer meeyeez
I'd like to leave these in your safe.	**Bunları kasanıza bırakmak istiyorum.**	boonlahrı kahssahnızah bırahkmahk eesteeyoroom
Can you find me a babysitter?	**Bana bir çocuk bakıcısı bulabilir misiniz?**	bahnah beer chojook bahkıjıssı boolahbeeleer meesseeneez

HOTEL SERVICE

May I have a/an/ some...?	... istiyorum.	... eesteeyoroom
ashtray	Bir küllük	beer kewllewk
bath towel	Bir banyo havlusu	beer bahnyo hahvloossoo
extra blanket	Bir battaniye (daha)	beer bahttahneeyeh (dahhah)
envelopes	Birkaç zarf	beerkahch zahrf
(more) hangers	Birkaç askı (daha)	beerkahch ahskı (dahhah)
ice cubes	Buz	booz
extra pillow	Bir yastık daha	beer yahstık dahhah
reading-lamp	Bir gece lambası	beer gᵛehjeh lahmbahssı
soap	Sabun	sahboon
writing paper	Mektup kâğıdı	mehktoop kᵛardı

Where's the...?	... nerededir?	... nehrehdehdeer
barber's	Erkek berberi	ehrkehk behrbehree
bathroom	Banyo	bahnyo
beauty salon	Güzellik salonu	gᵛewzehlleek sahlonoo
dining-room	Yemek salonu	yehmehk sahlonoo
hairdresser's	Kuaför	kooahfur
restaurant	Lokanta	lokahntah
television room	Televizyon odası	tehlehveezyon odahssı
toilet	Tuvalet	toovahleht

Breakfast

The Turkish breakfast consists of eggs, white cheese, olives, bread, butter and jam served with tea or milk. Some hotels can now also provide an English or American breakfast. Hot or cold cereals are only offered in luxury or first-class hotels. Don't forget that Moslem law forbids the eating of pork so bacon or ham will be hard to find on a breakfast menu.

I'll have an/some...	... istiyorum.	... eesteeyoroom
bacon and eggs	Jambonlu yumurta	zhahmbonloo yoomoortah
eggs	Yumurta	yoomoortah
boiled eggs	Haşlanmış yumurta	hashlahnmısh yoo-moortah
soft/medium/hard	çiğ/rafadan/kayısı	chee/rahfahdahn/kahyıssı
fried eggs	Sahanda yumurta	sahhahndah yoomoortah

fruit juice	**Meyve suyu**	mehyveh sooyoo
grapefruit/orange	**Greyfurt/Portakal**	greyfoort/portahkahl
pineapple/tomato	**Ananas/Domates**	ahnahnahss/domahtehss
ham and eggs	**Jambonlu yumurta**	zhahmbonloo yoomoortah
jam	**Reçel**	rehchehl
marmalade	**Marmelat**	mahrmehlaht
olives	**Zeytin**	zehyteen
omelet	**Omlet**	omleht
pancakes	**Ponçik**	poncheek
toast	**Tost**	tost
yoghurt	**Yoğurt**	yoroort
white cheese	**Beyaz peynir**	behyahz pehyneer
May I have some...	**... istiyorum.**	...eesteeyoroom
hot/cold milk	**Sıcak/Soğuk süt**	sıjahk/sorook sewt
cream/sugar	**Krema/Şeker**	krehmah/shehkehr
bread/rolls	**Ekmek/Küçük ekmek**	ehkmehk/kewchewk ehkmehk
butter	**Yağ**	yah
salt/pepper	**Tuz/Biber**	tooz/beebehr
coffee/tea	**Kahve/Çay**	kahhveh/chahy
chocolate	**Çikolata**	cheekolahtah
lemon/honey	**Limon/Bal**	leemon/bahl
hot water	**Sıcak su**	sıjahk soo
Could you bring me a...?	**Bana bir ... getirir misiniz?**	bahnah beer ... g^yehteereer meesseeneez
plate	**tabak**	tahbahk
glass/cup	**bardak/tas**	bahrdahk/tahss
knife/fork	**bıçak/çatal**	bıchahk/chahtahl
spoon	**kaşık**	kahshık

Difficulties

The ... doesn't work.	**... çalışmıyor.**	... chahlıshmıyor
air-conditioner	**Klima cihazı**	kleemah jıhahzı
fan	**Vantilatör**	vahnteelahturr
heating	**Kalorifer**	kahloreefehr
light	**Işık**	ıshık
radio	**Radyo**	rahdyo
tap	**Musluk**	mooslook
toilet	**Tuvalet**	toovahleht
ventilator	**Aspiratör**	ahspeerahturr

The wash-basin is clogged.	**Lavabo tıkalı.**	lahvahbo tıkahlı
The window is jammed.	**Pencere sıkışmış.**	pehnjehreh sıkıshmısh
The blind is stuck.	**Stor sıkışmış.**	stor sıkıshmısh
These aren't my shoes.	**Bunlar benim ayakkabılarım değil.**	boonlahr behneem ahyahkkahbılahrım deheel
This isn't my laundry.	**Bunlar benim çamaşırlarım değil.**	boonlahr behneem chamahshırlahrım deheel
There's no hot water.	**Sıcak su yok.**	sıjahk soo yok
I've lost my watch.	**Saatimi kaybettim.**	sahtımı kahybehtteem
I've left my key in my room.	**Anahtarımı odamda bıraktım.**	ahnahhtahrımı odahmdah bırahktım
The ... is broken.	**... kırıldı.**	... kırıldı
bulb	**Ampul**	ahmpool
lamp	**Lamba**	lahmbah
plug	**Priz**	preez
shutter	**Kepenk**	kehpehnk
switch	**Elektrik düğmesi**	ehlehtreek dewmehssee
venetian blind	**Stor**	stor
Can you get it repaired?	**Tamir ettirebilir misiniz?**	tahmeer ehtteerehbeeleer meesseeneez

Telephone—Mail—Callers

Can you get me Izmir 12345?	**İzmir 12345 i bağlar mısınız?**	eezmeer 12345 ee barlahr mıssınız
Did anyone telephone me?	**Bana telefon eden oldu mu?**	bahnah tehlehfon ehdehn oldoo moo
Do you have any stamps?	**Pul var mı?**	pool vahr mı
Would you please mail this for me?	**Bunu benim için postaya verir misiniz?**	boonoo behneem eecheen posstahyah vehreer meesseeneez
Are there any messages for me?	**Bana mesaj var mı?**	bahnah mehssahzh vahr mı

FOR POST OFFICE and TELEPHONE, see pages 137–141

Checking out

May I please have my bill?	Hesabı istiyorum, lütfen.	hehssahbı eesteeyoroom lewtfehn
I'm leaving early tomorrow. Please have my bill ready.	Yarın sabah erkenden hareket ediyorum. Lütfen hesabımı hazırlayın.	yahrın sahbahh ehrkehndehn hahrehkeht ehdeeyoroom. lewtfehn hehssahbımı hahzırlahyın
We'll be checking out around noon/soon.	Öğleye doğru/ Hemen hareket edeceğiz.	urleyeh dorroo/hehmehn hahrehkeht ehdehjeheez
I must leave at once.	Hemen hareket etmeliyim.	hehmehn hahrehkeht ehtmehleeyeem
Is everything included?	Herşey dahil mi?	hehrshey dahheel mee
You've made a mistake in this bill, I think.	Zannedersem bu hesapta bir hata yaptınız.	zahnnehdehrsem boo hehssahptah beer hahtah yahptınız
Can you get us a taxi?	Bize bir taksi çağırır mısınız?	beezeh beer tahksee chahrırmıssınız
When's the next... to Izmir?	İzmir'e gidecek ... ne zaman?	eezmeere gᵉeedehjehk ... neh zahmahn
bus/train/plane	otobüs/tren/uçak	otobewss/trehn/oochahk
Would you send someone to bring down our baggage?	Bagajlarımızı indirmeye birisini yollar mısınız?	bahhahzhlahrımızı eendeermehyeh beereesseenee yollahr mıssınız
We're in a great hurry.	Çok acelemiz var.	chok ahjehlehmeez vahr
Here's the forwarding address.	İşte gideceğimiz yerin adresi.	eeshteh gᵉeedehjeheeemeez yehreen ahdrehssee
You have my home address.	Sizde ev adresim var.	seezdeh ehv ahdrehsseem vahr
It's been a very enjoyable stay.	Burada çok hoş zaman geçirdik.	boorahdah chock hosh zahmahn gᵉehcheerdeek
I hope we'll come again sometime.	Birgün yine geleceğimizi ümit ederim.	beergᵉewn yeeneh gᵉehlehjeheeemeezee ewmeet ehdehreem

FOR TAXI, see page 27

HOTEL SERVICE

Eating out

There are several types of places which serve food in Turkey

Lokanta
(lokahntah)

Some restaurants display a "touris menu" in English and other lan guages and, in addition, offer one o more set menus. These restaurant have been rated first or second clas by the ministry of tourism, bu there's no appreciable difference be tween the two classes. There are othe good restaurants which cater to loca clientele where the menus are only in Turkish, or there's no menu at all

Kebapçı
(kehbahpchı)

A restaurant serving *kebap*—kebobs shishkebobs or other grilled meats

Köfteci
(kurftehjee)

A restaurant specializing in *köfte*, type of grilled croquette made o minced lamb. It's often served wit a string-bean salad garnished wit chopped onions and hard-boiled eggs

İşkembeci
(eeshkehmbehjee)

A restaurant specializing in *işkemb çorbası* (a mutton tripe soup).

Pideci
(peedehjee)

Popular on the northern coast o Turkey, a *pideci* comes close to being a pizza parlour. It serves a flat bread *(pide)* hot out of the oven and gar nished with minced meat, tomatoe and/or cheese.

Muhallebici
(moohahllehbeejee)

You'll find a large variety of loca pastries available here plus dairy des serts like custard pudding.

Büfe
(bewfeh)

Chicken is among the popular snacks offered along with soft drinks and other light fare.

Gazino
(gahzeeno)

A type of family supper club where you can be entertained with Near Eastern music and dances while dining.

Eating habits

Turkish cooking is characterized by its grilled meats, savoury stuffed vegetables and pastry desserts steeped in syrup. Shish-kebob, stuffed grape leaves and baklava are among the scores of preparations which epicureans around the world enjoy.

Though major cities will have a selection of foreign restaurants, you shouldn't pass up the opportunity of sampling the simple but tasty local dishes. They represent a style of cooking common throughout the Mediterranean region.

Moslem law restrains the drinking of alcoholic beverages. Nevertheless, you'll probably be able to order beer, wine or *rakı* (an aniseed liqueur) with your meal. By the way, Moslem law forbids the eating of pork but it may be offered in foreign restaurants.

If you seem the slightest bit perplexed about what you want to eat, don't be surprised if the waiter leads you right into the kitchen. You can then choose your meal from a dozen or so saucepans. But if the waiter doesn't invite you, just ask him if you can step into the kitchen to choose your food. This practice is very common throughout the country except in high-class or foreign restaurants.

| May we choose our food from the kitchen? | **Yemeğimizi mutfaktan seçebilir miyiz?** | yehmeheemeezee mootfahktahn sehchehbeeleer meeyeez |

EATING OUT

Meal times

We assume you've already had your breakfast (*kahvaltı*—kahh**vahl**tı) at the hotel. If not, turn to pages 34 and 35 for a breakfast menu.

Lunch (*öğle yemeği*—ew**leh** yehme**hee**) is served between noon and 2 p.m., while dinner (*akşam yemeği*—ahk**shahm** yehme**hee**) is served from 7 to 10 p.m.

Hungry?

I'm hungry/I'm thirsty.	**Acıktım/Susadım.**	ah**jık**tım/soos**sah**dım
Can you recommend a good restaurant?	**İyi bir lokanta tavsiye edebilir misiniz?**	ee**yee** beer lo**kahn**tah tahv**see**yeh ehdeh**bee**leer mees**see**neez
Are there any inexpensive restaurants around here?	**Civarda ucuz lokantalar var mı?**	jivahr**dah** oo**jooz** lo**kahn**tah**lahr** vahr mı

If you want to be sure of getting a table in a well-known restaurant, it may be better to telephone in advance.

I'd like to reserve a table for four.	**Dört kişilik yer rezerve ettirmek istiyorum.**	durt kee**shee**leek yehr reh**zehr**veh eht**teer**mehk ees**tee**yoroom
We'll come at 8.	**Saat 8 de geleceğiz.**	sart 8 deh g^yehleh**jeh**heez

Asking and ordering

Good evening. I'd like a table for three.	İyi akşamlar. Üç kişilik bir masa istiyorum.	eeyee ahkshahmlahr. ewch keesheeleek beer mahssah eesteeyoroom
Could we have a...?	... bir masa var mı?	... beer mahssah vahr mı
table in the corner	Köşede	kurshehdeh
table by the window	Pencere kenarında	pehnjehreh kehnahrındah
table outside	Dışarıda	dıshahrıdah
table on the terrace	Taraçada	tahrahchahdah
May I please have the menu?	Menüyü görebilir miyim?	mehnewyew gurrehbeeleer meeyeem
What's this?	Bu nedir?	boo nehdeer
Do you have...?	... bulunur mu?	... booloonoor moo
a set menu	Tabldot	tahbldot
local dishes	Yerli yemekler	yehrlee yehmehklehr
Is service included?	Servis dahil midir?	sehrveess dahheel meedeer
Could we have (a/an) ..., please?	Bir ... istiyorum, lütfen?	beer...eesteeyoroom lewtfehn
ashtray	küllük	kewllewk
another chair	başka sandalye	bahshkah sahndahlyeh
glass	bardak	bahrdahk
knife	bıçak	bıchahk
napkin	peçete	pehchehteh
plate	tabak	tahbahk
serviette	peçete	pehchehteh
spoon	kaşık	kahshık
toothpick	kürdan	kewrdahn

EATING OUT

Ne arzu edersiniz?	What would you like?
Bunu tavsiye ederim.	I recommend this.
İçecek olarak ne arzu edersiniz?	What would you like to drink?
Bizde...yok.	We haven't got...
...istermisiniz?	Do you want...?

I'd like a/an/some...	... istiyorum.	...eesteeyoroom
aperitif	Aperitif	ahpehreeteef
appetizer	Ordövr	ordurvr
beer	Bira	beerah
bread	Ekmek	ehkmehk
butter	Tereyağı	tehrehyahrı
cabbage	Lâhana	larhahnah
chips	Patates kızartması	pahtahtehss kızahrtmahssı
cheese	Peynir	payneer
coffee	Kahve	kahhveh
dessert	Tatlılar	tahtlılahr
fish	Balık	bahlık
french fries	Patates kızartması	pahtahtehss kızahrtmahssı
fruit	Meyve	mayveh
game	Av eti	ahv ehtee
ice-cream	Dondurma	dondoormah
ketchup	Keçap	kehchahp
lemon	Limon	leemon
lettuce	Marul	mahrool
meat	Et	eht
mineral water	Maden suyu	mahdehn sooyoo
milk	Süt	sewt
mustard	Hardal	hahrdahl
oil	Yağ	yar
olive oil	Zeytinyağı	zayteenyarı
pepper	Karabiber	kahrahbeebehr
potatoes	Patates	pahtahtehss
poultry	Kümes hayvanları	kewmehss hahyvahnlahrı
rice	Pirinç	peereench
rolls	Sandöviç ekmeği	sahndurveech ehkmehree
salad	Salata	sahlahtah
salt	Tuz	tooz
sandwich	Sandviç	sahndveech
seafood	Deniz mahsulleri	dehneez mahhssoollehree
seasoning	Baharat	bahhahraht
soup	Çorba	chorbah
spaghetti	Spagetti	spahgvehttee
starter	Ordövr	ordurvr
sugar	Şeker	shehkehr
tea	Çay	chahy
vegetables	Sebzeler	sehbzehlehr
vinegar	Sirke	seerkeh
(iced) water	(Buzlu) su	(boozloo) soo
wine	Şarap	shahrahp

What's on the menu?

Our menu is presented according to courses. Under the headings below you'll find alphabetical lists of dishes that might be offered on a Turkish menu with their English equivalents. You can also show the book to the waiter. If you want a vegetable, for instance, show him the appropriate list and let *him* point at what's available. Use pages 41 and 42 for ordering in general.

Here then is our guide to good eating and drinking. Turn to the section you want.

Obviously, you're not going to go through every course on the menu. If you've had enough, say:

Nothing more, thanks.	**Başka birşey istemiyorum, teşekkürler.**	bahsh**kah** beer**shehy** eestehmee**yo**room teh-shehk**kewr**lehr

EATING OUT

Appetizers

I'd like an appetizer.	Ordövr istiyorum.	ordurvr eesteeyoroom
What do you recommend ?	Ne tavsiye edersiniz ?	neh tahvsseeyeh ehdehrsseeneez
ançuez	ahnchooehz	anchovies
arnavut ciğeri	ahrnahvoot jeeehree	spiced mutton liver
beyin tavası	behyeen tahvahssı	fried lamb brains
çiroz salatası	cheeroz sahlahtahssı	cured mackerel salad
deniz mahsulleri kokteyli	dehneez mahhsoollehree koktaylee	seafood cocktail
dil	deel	ox tongue
füme/süğüş	fewmeh/surewsh	smoked/boiled
enginar	ehngʸeenahr	marinated artichoke
fava	fahvah	mashed fava beans
havyar	hahvyahr	caviar
humus	hoomooss	mashed chick-peas
ıstakoz (ızgara)	ıstahkoz (ızgahrah)	(grilled) lobster
istiridye	eesteereedyeh	oysters
karides (kokteyli)	kahreedehss (koktaylee)	shrimp (cocktail)
kılıç balığı füme	kılıch bahlıı fewmeh	smoked swordfish
kuru fasulye piyaz	kooroo fahssoolyeh peeyahz	butter-bean salad
kuzu	koozoo	lamb
ciğeri	jeeehree	liver
beyin salatası	behyeen sahlahtahssı	brain salad
lâkerda	larkehrdah	tinned tunny (canned tuna)
mersin balığı füme	mehrseen bahlıı fewmeh	smoked sturgeon
midye	meedyeh	mussels
pavurya	pahvooryah	crab
sardalya	sahrdahlyah	sardines
tarama	tahrahmah	creamed red caviar
ton balığı	ton bahlıı	tunny fish (tuna)
turşu	toorshoo	pickled vegetables
zeytin	zehyteen	olives
siyah/yeşil	seeyah/yehsheel	black/green

Here are some appetizers you'll want to try:

çerkez tavuğu (chehrkehz tahvoo)	chicken Circassian; minced chicken mixed with chopped walnuts, chili pepper and bread
midye dolması (meedyeh dolmahssı)	minced mussels with rice and onion and served on the half-shell

| **astırma**
(pahsstırmah) | dried beef cured with red pepper; Turkish pastrami |
| **eytinyağlı dolmalar**
(zehyteenyahlı dolmahlahr) | eggplant, grape leaves or green pepper stuffed with rice, raisins and pistachios; served chilled |

Salads

What salads do you have ?	**Salata olarak neleriniz var ?**	sahlahtah olahrahk nehlehreeneez vahr
oban salatası	chobahn sahlahtahssı	cucumber and tomato salad
avuç salatası	hahvooch sahlahtahssı	carrot salad
arışık salata	kahrıshık sahlahtah	mixed salad
arışık turşu	kahrıshık toorshoo	pickled vegetables
ereviz salatası	kehrehveez sahlahtahssı	celery salad
narul salatası	mahrool sahlahtahssı	romaine lettuce salad
nevsim salatası	mehvseem sahlahtahssı	salad of the season
ancar salatası	pahnjahr sahlahtahssı	beetroot salad
atlıcan salatası	pahtlıjahn sahlahtahssı	aubergine (eggplant) salad
us salatası	rooss sahlahtahssı	diced vegetable salad
eşil salata	yehsheel sahlahtah	green salad

We recommend you try this salad :

| **acık**
(jahjik) | diced cucumbers with a dressing of yogurt, olive oil and garlic |

Egg dishes and omelets

d like an omelet.	**Bir omlet istiyorum.**	beer omleht eesteeyoroom
ılbır	chılbır	poached eggs with yoghurt
aşlanmışyumurta	hahshlahnmısh yoomoortah	boiled eggs
mlet	omleht	omelet
antarlı omlet	mahntarlı omleht	mushroom omelet
aydanozlu omlet	mahydahnozloo omleht	parsley omelet
eynirli omlet	pehyneerlee omleht	cheese omelet

| **nenemen**
(mehnehmehn) | spicy omelet with green peppers and tomatoes |

Soups

I'd like some soup.	**Çorba istiyorum.**	chorbah eesteeyoroom
What do you recommend?	**Ne tavsiye edersiniz?**	neh tahvseeyeh ehdehrseeneez
bezelye çorbası	behzehlyeh chorbahssı	pea soup
borç	borch	borsch
domates çorbası	domahtehss chorbahssı	tomato soup
domatesli pirinç çorbası	domahtehsslee peereench chorbahssı	tomato and rice soup
ekmek çorbası	ehkmehk chorbahssı	bread soup
erişteli çorba	ehreeshtehlee chorbah	noodle soup
et suyu (konsome)	eht sooyoo (konsomeh)	consommé
gratine soğan çorbası	grahteeneh soahn chorbahssı	French onion soup
irmik çorbası	eermeek chorbahssı	semolina soup
kırmızı mercimek çorbası	kırmızı mehrjeemehk chorbahssı	red lentil soup
kremalı domates çorbası	krehmahlı domahtehss chorbahssı	cream of tomato
mercimek çorbası	mehrjeemehk chorbahssı	lentil soup
sebze çorbası	sehbzeh chorbahssı	vegetable soup
soğuk et suyu	sooook eht sooyoo	chilled consommé
tavuk suyu	tahvook sooyoo	chicken consommé
taze mısır çorbası	tahzeh mıssır chorbahssı	maize (corn) soup
yayla çorbası	yahylah chorbahssı	mutton soup creamed with yoghurt

Here are some soup specialities from the Turkish cuisine:

işkembe çorbası (eeshkehmbeh chorbahssı)	mutton tripe soup; made of vinegar, garlic, red pepper and often eggs; Turks say it's good remedy for a hangover
düğün çorbası (dewewn chorbahssı)	"wedding soup"; lamb soup flavoured with lemon juice and thickened with beaten egg
tarhana çorbası (tahrhahnah chorbahssı)	yoghurt soup made with flour, tomatoes and pimentos

Fish and seafood

I'd like some fish.	**Balık istiyorum.**	bahlık eesteeyoroom
What kinds of seafood do you have?	**Deniz mahsullerinden neler var?**	dehneez mahhsoollehreendehn nehlehr vahr
alabalık	ahlahbahlık	trout
barbunya	bahrboonyah	red mullet
çinakop	cheenahkop	variety of seabass
dil balığı	deel bahlıı	sole
gümüş	grewmewsh	small silverfish
hamsi	hahmsee	spratts
ıstakoz	ıstahkoz	lobster
kalkan	kahlkahn	turbot
karides	kahreedehss	prawns
tavası	tahvahssı	sautéed
kefal	kehfahl	grey mullet
kılıç balığı	kılıch bahlıı	swordfish
lâkerda	larkehrdah	salted tunny (tuna)
levrek	lehvrehk	seabass
kâğıtta	karıttah	baked in a parchment envelope
mantarlı	mahntahrlı	baked with mushrooms in a parchment envelope
mayonezli	mahyonehzlee	with mayonnaise
tavası	tahvahssı	sautéed
lüfer	lewfehr	a type of seabass
mercan	mehrjahn	bream
mersin balığı	mehrsseen bahlıı	sturgeon
midye	meedyeh	mussels
tavası	tahvahssı	sautéed
pilâkisi	peelarkeessee	braised with vegetables
palamut	pahlahmoot	tunny (tuna)
pisi	peessee	brill
sardalya	sahrdahlyah	sardines
sazan	sahzahn	carp
tekir	tehkeer	barbel
torik	toreek	tunny (tuna)
turna	toornah	pike
uskumru	ooskoomroo	mackerel
dolması	dolmahssı	stuffed and fried
yılan balığı	yılahn bahlıı	eel

You'll especially enjoy this swordfish shishkebob if you're at the seaside:

kılıç şiş (kılıch sheesh)	Chunks of swordfish skewered and charcoal-grilled with bay leaves, tomatoes and green peppers
çınarcık usulü balık (chınahrjık oossoolew bahlık)	A preparation of swordfish, seabass and prawns. The dish is fried and served up garnished with mushrooms and flavoured with brandy.
lüfer firim (lewfehr feereem)	Seabass baked with parsley. The fish is served chilled and garnished with olives and lemon and diced gherkins, carrots and egg.

Here are two more mouth-watering fish dishes typical of Turkey that you'll find on many restaurant menus:

There are many ways of preparing fish. Here are the translations of the ways you may want it served:

baked	**fırında**	fırındah
braised	**pilâki**	peelarkee
fried	**tavada kızarmış**	tahvahdah kızahrmısh
deep fried	**yağda kızarmış**	yardah kızahrmısh
grilled	**ızgara**	ızgahrah
marinated	**salamura**	sahlahmoorah
poached	**haşlama**	hahshlahmah
raw	**çiğ**	chee
smoked	**füme**	fewmeh
steamed	**buğulama**	boolahmah

Meat

'd like some...	... istiyorum.	... eesteeyoroom
beef/pork	**Sığır/Domuz**	sıır/domooz
veal/lamb	**Dana/Kuzu**	dahnah/koozoo
Iman bifteği	ahlmahn beeftehee	hamburger steak
bahçıvan köftesi	bahhchıvahn kurftehssee	meat croquettes with potatoes and egg-plant
beğendili kebap	behehndeelee kehbahp	lamb kebobs with eggplant purée
beyinli patlıcan kebabı	behyeenlee pahtlıjahn kehbahbı	lamb stew with brains and eggplant
çoban kebabı	chobahn kehbahbı	mutton braised with garlic
Dana budu rosto	dahnah boodoo rosto	leg of veal
Dana rozbif	dahnah rozbeef	roast veal
düğün eti	dewewn ehtee	mutton stew called "Turkish wedding meat"
içli köfte	eechlee kurfteh	stuffed mutton cro-quettes
işkembe dolması	eeshkehmbeh dolmahssı	mutton tripe stuffed with rice and liver
islim kebabı	eesleem kehbahbı	lamb stew with vegetables
ızgara köfte	ızgahrah kurfteh	grilled meat croquettes
İzmir köftesi	eezmeer kurftehssee	lamb croquettes in gravy
kâğıt kebabı	karıt kahbahbı	lamb kebobs in a parchment envelope
kapama	kahpahmah	lamb stew with spring onions
kuzu	koozoo	lamb
budu rosto sebzeli	boodoo rosto sehb-zehlee	leg of lamb braised with vegetables
dolması	dolmahssı	lamb stuffed with savoury rice, liver and pistachios
güveç	gʸewvehch	casserole
haşlama	hahshlahmah	stew
tas kebabı	tahss kehbahbı	lamb kebobs in a casserole
tandır	tahndır	roasted in a cylindrical oven

nohutlu işkembe	nohootloo eeshkehmbeh	tripe with chick-peas
patlıcan kebabı	pahtlıjahn kehbahbı	lamb kebobs with eggplant
salçalı köfte	sahlchahlı kurfteh	meat croquettes in tomato sauce
sebzeli rozbif	sehbzehlee rozbeef	roast beef with vegetables
sığır Stroganof	sıır strogahnof	beef Stroganof
şiş köfte	sheesh kurfteh	skewered lamb croquettes
soğanlı biftek, Viyana usûlü	soahnlı beeftehk veeyahnah oossoolew	steak with browned onions
tencere kebabı	tehnjehreh kehbahbı	mutton stew with peas and potatoes
terbiyeli köfte	tehrbeeyehlee kurfteh	rice and meatballs cooked and served with a light sauce
terbiyeli kuzu eti	tehrbeeyehlee koozoo ehtee	lamb with lemon dressing
terbiyeli paça	tehrbeeyehlee pahchah	lamb shank
yumurta köftesi	voomoortah kurftehssee	meat croquettes stuffed with eggs

Meat dishes

We recommend you try...

döner kebap
(durnehr kehbahp)

leg of lamb roasted on a vertical spit from which thin slices are cut and served on a bed of rice

hünkâr beğendi
(hewnkarr behehndee)

minced lamb served on an eggplant purée, literally called "His Majesty enjoys it"

kadın budu köfte
(kahdın boodoo kurfteh)

"lady's thigh" is the name given to lamb and rice croquettes, generally served with chips (french fries)

şiş kababı
(sheesh kehbahbı)

shishkebob; charcoal-grilled skewered chunks of lamb and tomatoes

How do you like your meat?

baked	fırında	fırındah
spit roasted	çevirme	chehveermeh
boiled	haşlama	hahshlahmah
broiled	ızgara	ısgahrah
casserole	tencerede pişmiş	tehnjehrehdeh peeshmeesh
fried	tavada kızarmış	tahvahdah kızahrmısh
grilled	ızgara	ızgahrah
roasted	rosto	rossto
stewed	yahni	yahhnee
stuffed	dolma	dolmah
underdone (rare)	az pişmiş	ahz peeshmeesh
medium	orta pişmiş	ortah peeshmeesh
well-done	iyi pişmiş	eeyee peeshmeesh

Game and fowl

bıldırcın	bıldırjın	quail
çil	cheel	partridge
çulluk	choollook	woodcock
keklik	kehkleek	red partridge
sülün	sewlewn	pheasant
tavşan	tahvshahn	hare
yaban domuzu paçası	yahbahn domoozoo pahchahssı	wild boar
yabani kaz	yahbahnee kahz	wild duck
yabani ördek	yahbahnee urrdehk	wild goose

Poultry

hindi kızartması/ dolması iç pilâvı	heendee kızahrtmahssı/dolmahssı eech peelahvı	turkey roast/stuffed with seasoned rice
kâğıtta piliç	karıttah peeleech	chicken baked in a parchment envelope
kaz kızartması	kahz kızahrtmahssı	roast goose
ördek kızartması	urrdehk kızahrtmahssı	roast duckling
piliç	peeleech	chicken
sebzeli piliç güveci	sehbzehlee peeleech gᵞewvehjee	chicken and vegetable stew
sebzeli tavuk haşlaması	sehbzehlee tahvuhk hahshlahmahssı	chicken braised with vegetables
tavuk haşlaması	tahvook hahshlahmahssı	boiled chicken

Vegetables

What vegetables do you recommend?	Sebze olarak ne tavsiye edersiniz?	sehbzeh olahrahk neh tahvseeyeh ehdherseeneez
I'd prefer some salad.	Salata tercih ederim.	sahlahtah tehrjeeh ehdehreem
bakla yoğurtlu	bahklah yooortloo	fava beans with yoghurt
bezelye	behzehlyeh	green peas
biber	beebehr	green peppers
Brüksel lâhanası	brewksehl larhahnahssı	brussels sprouts
enginar	ehngveenahr	artichoke
havuç	hahvooch	carrots
ıspanak	ıspahnahk	spinach
kabak	kahbahk	vegetable marrow (zucchini)
karnıbahar	kahrnıbahhahr	cauliflower
kereviz	kehrehveez	celery
kuşkonmaz	kooshkonmahz	asparagus
lâhana	larhahnah	cabbage
patlıcan	pahtlıjahn	aubergine (eggplant)
pilâki	peelarkee	navy beans in oil
prasa	prahssah	leeks
taze fasulye	tahzeh fahssoolyeh	green beans
zeytinyağlı barbunya	zehyteenyahlı bahrboonyah	red haricot beans
zeytinyağlı çalı fasulye	zehyteenyahlı chahlı fahssoolyeh	french beans, green beans
zeytinyağlı fasulye	zehyteenyahlı fahssoolyeh	string beans
zeytinyağlı kızartmalar	zehyteenyahlı kızahrtmahlahr	vegetables with yoghurt or tomato sauce

Vegetables may be served:

baked	fırında	fırındah
boiled	haşlama	hahshlahmah
chopped	kıyılmış	kıyılmısh
creamed	kremalı	krehmahlı
diced	doğranmış	dohrahnmısh
fried	tavada kızarmış	tahvahdah kızahrmısh
grilled	ızgara	ızgahrah
roasted	kızarmış	kızahrmısh
stewed	yahni usulü	yahhnee oossoolew
stuffed	dolma	dolmah

Turkish cooking is renowned for its variety of vegetables stuffed with a mixture of chopped meat (usually lamb or mutton), rice, onion and herbs. The name of *dolma* preceded by the word *zeytinyağlı* usually indicates that it's also filled with raisins and pistachios. These *domalar* may be eaten hot or cold and are usually served with yoghurt.

biber dolması	beebehr dolmahssı	stuffed peppers
domates dolması	domahtehss dolmahssı	stuffed tomatoes
kabak dolması	kahbahk dolmahssı	stuffed marrows (zucchini)
lâhana dolması	larhahnah dolmahssı	stuffed cabbage leaves
patlıcan dolması	pahtlıjahn dolmahssı	stuffed aubergine (eggplant)
yaprak dolması	yahprahk dolmahssı	stuffed grape leaves

Another variation of fried aubergine (eggplant) is filled with onions, parsley and tomatoes and served cold. It must have overwhelmed the epicurean palate of the mosque's religious leader since they call it *imam bayıldı* (ee**mahn** bahyıl**dı**)—which means "The priest fainted".

Pilaf and potatoes

You'll certainly want to try rice pilaf, a rice dish prepared in any one of countless ways.

bulgur pilavı	boolgoor peelahvı	cracked wheat pilaf
domatesli pilav	domahtehslee peelahv	tomato pilaf
ciğer pilav	eech peelahv	chopped chicken-liver pilaf
şehriyeli pilav	shehhreeyehlee peelahv	noodle pilaf
tavuklu pilav	tahvookloo peelahv	pilaf with diced chicken
tereyağlı pilav	tehrehyahlı peelahv	butter pilaf
ince pomfrit	eenjeh pomfreet	shoestring potatoes
patates	pahtahtehss	potatoes
kızartması	kızahrtmahssı	chips (french fried potatoes)
köftesi	kurftehssee	croquettes

Noodles and pasties

Börek is one of the specialities of Turkish cuisine, a type of pasty or pie. Though it can take different forms, it's made basically of puff pastry filled with chopped meat, cheese or vegetables.

arpa şehriyesi fırında	ahrpah shehhreeyehssee fırındah	baked oat noodles
erişte	ehreeshteh	noodles
ıspanaklı kuru börek	ıspahnahklı kooroo burrehk	spinach pie
kıymalı börek	kıymahlı burrehk	minced-meat pie
kıymalı makarna	kıymahlı mahkahrnah	macaroni with minced meat
makarna	mahkahrnah	macaroni
mantı	mahntı	ravioli
peynirli börek	pehyneerlee burrehk	cheese pie
salçalı makarna	sahlchahlı mahkahrnah	macaroni with tomato sauce
su böreği kıymalı	soo burrehee kıymahlı	minced-meat pie
su böreği peynirli	soo burrehee pehyneerlee	cheese pie
talaş kebabı	tahlash kahbahbı	meat pie
tatar böreği	tahtahr burrehee	minced-meat pie
tavuklu börek	tahvookloo burrehk	chicken pie

Cheese

It isn't customary to have a cheese course in Turkey. Besides some imitations of well-known European cheeses, here are some Turkish varieties:

beyaz peynir (behyahz pehyneer)	white cheese, not unlike the famous Greek *feta* cheese
çerkez peyniri (chehrkehz pehyneeree)	a creamy cheese
kaşer peyniri (kahshehr pehyneeree)	a firm, yellowish cheese
tulum peyniri (tooloom pehyneeree)	a salty goat's milk cheese

Dessert

If you've survived all the courses on the menu, you may want to say:

I'd like a dessert, please.	**Bir tatlı istiyorum, lütfen.**	beer tahtlı eesteeyoroom lewtfehn
Something light, please.	**Hafif bir şey, lütfen.**	hah**feef** beer shehy lewt**fehn**
Just a small portion.	**Sadece küçük bir porsiyon.**	sah**deh**jeh kew**chewk** beer por**see**yon
Nothing more, thanks.	**Başka birşey istemiyorum, teşekkürler.**	bahsh**kah** beershehy eestehmeeyoroom tehshehk**kewr**lehr

If you aren't sure what to order, ask the waiter:

What do you have for dessert?	**Tatlı olarak neleriniz var?**	tahtlı olah**rahk** nehleh**ree**neez vahr
What do you recommend?	**Ne tavsiye edersiniz?**	neh tahv**see**yeh ehdehr**see**neez

Turks have a sweet tooth for gooey, syrupy desserts like the well-known *baklava*. Some desserts even bear titillating names like "sweetheart's lips" or "lady's navel". And you'll be intrigued about eating the "vizier's finger" or a "nightingale's nest". Here are some Turkish favourites:

aşure (ah**shoo**reh)	"Noah's pudding"; thick pudding with fruit, nuts, vegetables
baba tatlısı (bah**bah** tahtlıssı)	savarin; ring-shaped cake with a centre filling of custard or fruits; macerated in syrup
baklava (bahk**lah**vah)	baklava; pastry filled with nuts, almonds and pistachios, steeped in syrup
bülbül yuvası (bewl**bewl** yoovahssı)	"nightingale's nest"; pastry filled with pistachio and walnut purée served with water ice (sherbet)
dilber dudağı (deel**behr** doodahı)	"sweetheart's lips"; pastry filled with pistachios and other nuts
kabak tatlısı (kah**bahk** tahtlıssı)	pumpkin served with nuts and water ice (sherbet)

dondurma şantiyeli	dondoormah shahnteeyhelee	ice-cream with whipped cream
ekmek kadayıfı	ehkmehk kahdahyıfı	pudding steeped in syrup
frape	frahpeh	milkshake
güllaç tatlısı	gyewllahch tahtlıssı	rose-flavoured pudding
irmik helvası	eermeek hehlvahssı	semolina-sugar confection
karışık dondurma	kahrıshık dondoormah	assorted ice-cream
karışık hamur tatlıları	kahrıshık hahmoor tahtlılahrı	assorted pastries
kaymaklı ve sütlü dondurma	kahymahklı veh sewtlew dondoormah	ice-cream
kazan dibi	kahzahn deebee	pudding with caramelized bottom
komposto	komposto	stewed fruit
krem şokola	krehm shokolah	chocolate pudding
krem karamel	krehm kahrahmehl	flan
krep süzet	krehp sewzeht	jam-filled pancakes
meyvalı dondurma	mehyvahlı dondoormah	water ice (sherbet)
meyveli tartlet	mehyvehlee tahrtleht	fruit tart
meyve salatası (likörlü/kremalı)	mehyveh sahlahtahssı (leekurlew/krehmahlı)	fruit cocktail (with liqueur/cream)
meyveli turta	mehyvehlee toortah	fruit cake
muhallebi	moohahllehbee	rice pudding
peşmelba	pehshmehlbah	peach melba
revâni	rehvahnee	semolina pudding
şekerpâre	shehkehrpahreh	water ice (sherbet) on a cake square
strudel	stroodhel	apple strudel
sufle	soofleh	soufflé
sütlaç	sewtlach	rice pudding
tavuk göğsü	tahvook gurssew	sweet chicken-breast mould
turtalar	toortahlahr	tarts
yoğurt	yooort	yoghurt

That's the end of our Turkish menu. For wine and other drinks, see the next pages. But after the feast comes...

The bill (check)

I'd like to pay.	Ödeyebilir miyim?	urdehyehbeeleer meeyeem
We'd like to pay separately.	Ayrı ayrı ödemek istiyoruz.	ahyrı ahyrı urdehmehk eesteeyorooz
You made a mistake in this bill, I think.	Zannedersem hesapta bir yanlışlık yaptınız.	zahnnehdehrsehm hehssaptah beer yahnlıshlık yahptınız
What's this amount for?	Toplam ne kadar tutuyor?	toplahm neh kahdahr tootooyor
Is everything included?	Herşey dahil mi?	hehrshehy dahheel mee
Do you accept traveller's cheques?	Seyahat çeki kabul ediyor musunuz?	sehyahhaht chehkee kahbool ehdeeyor moossoonooz
Thank you, this is for you.	Teşekkür ederim, bu da sizin için.	tehshehkkewr ehdehreem boo dah seezeen eecheen
Keep the change.	Bozuklar sizde kalsın.	bozooklahr seezdeh kahlsın
That was a very good meal.	Bu iyi bir yemekti.	boo eeyee beer yehmehktee
We enjoyed it, thank you.	Memnun kaldık, teşekkür ederiz.	mehmnoon kahldık tehshehkkewr ehdehreez

> **SERVİS DAHİLDİR**
> SERVICE INCLUDED

Complaints

But perhaps you'll have something to complain about:

That's not what I ordered. I asked for...	Söylediğim bu değil. Ben... istemistim.	surlehdeem boo deheel. behn ... eestehmeeshteem.
May I change this?	Bunu değiştirebilir miyim?	boonoo deheeshteerehbeeleer meeyèem
The meat is...	Et ...	eht
overdone/underdone	çok pişmiş/az pişmiş	chok peeshmeesh/ahz peeshmeesh
too tough	sert	sehrt

This is too...	**Bu çok...**	boo **chok**
bitter / salty / sweet	**acı/tuzlu/tatlı**	**ahj**ı/**toozloo**/**tahtl**ı
The food is cold.	**Yemek soğuk.**	**yehmehk soook**
This isn't fresh.	**Bu taze değil.**	boo **tahzeh deheel**
What's taking you so long?	**Bu gecikmenin sebebi ne?**	boo g**ᵛehjeekmehneen sehbehbee** neh
Where are our drinks?	**İçeceklerimiz nerede?**	**eechehjehklehreemeez nehrehdeh**
This isn't clean.	**Bu temiz değil.**	boo **tehmeez deheel**
Would you ask the head waiter to come over?	**Şef-garsonu çağırır-mısınız?**	shef **gahrsonoo chahrırmıssınız**

Drinks

Beer

You may be surprised to know that beer is perhaps the nation's most popular alcoholic beverage. Try these beers:

Efes-Pilsen	**ehfehs-peelsehn**	pilsner; light beer with a strong hops flavour
Tekel Altınbaşak	**tehkehl ahltıhnbahshahk**	may be light or dark
Tekel beyaz	**tehkehl behyahz**	light beer
Tekel siyah	**tehkehl seeyah**	dark beer
Tuborg	**toobohrg**	Turkish imitation of the famed Danish beer
I'd like a (cold) beer, please.	**(Soğuk) Bir bira istiyorum, lütfen.**	(**soook**) beer **beerah eesteeyoroom lewtfehn**

Wine

Because the drinking of alcoholic beverages is restricted for Moslems, wine isn't commonly drunk in Turkey. It's likely not to be available in small restaurants or outside cities. Nevertheless, wine production in this area goes back to ancient times. Some experts assert that the first grape vines were brought from Anatolia to Europe. Only a very small part of the grapes cultivated in Turkey are used to produce wine, and much of it is exported. Generally of a good quality, the best Turkish wine—particularly white—comes from the vicinity of Izmir while other wineyards are found in Thrace, around the Marmara coast and in Anatolia. Here are the names of some fine Turkish wines:

Adabağ	ahdahbah	red
Kalebağ	kahlehbah	red
Tekel Gaziantep	tehkehl gahzeeahntehp	red dessert wine
Tekel Kalebağ Ankara	tehkehl kahlehbah ahnkahrah	red dessert wine
Tekel Misbağ İzmir	tehkehl meesbah eezmeer	dry white

And here are a few good table wines:

Çubuk	choobook	red, dry white
Güzel Marmara	gʸewzehl mahrmahrah	red, dry to slightly dry white
Güzelbağ Marmara	gʸewzehlbah mahrmahrah	red, dry to slightly dry white
İzmir	eezmeer	red, dry white

I'd like...	... istiyorum.	... eesteeyoroom
a small carafe	Küçük bir sürahi	kewchewk beer sewrahhee
a bottle	Bir şişe	beer sheesheh
half a bottle	Yarım şişe	yahrim sheesheh
a glass	Bir bardak	beer bahrdahk
I'd like something...	... birşey istiyorum.	... beershay eesteeyoroom
sweet/sparkling/dry	Tatlı/Köpüklü/Sek	tahtlı/kurpewklew/sehk
I want a bottle of white wine/red wine.	Bir şişe beyaz şarap/kırmızı şarap istiyorum.	beer sheesheh behyahz shahrahp/kırmızı shahrahp eesteeyoroom
I don't want anything too sweet.	Fazla tatlı birşey istemiyorum.	fahzlah tahtlı beershay eestehmeeyoroom
How much is a bottle of...?	Bir şişe ... ne kadardır?	beer sheesheh ... neh kahdahrdır
Haven't you anything cheaper?	Daha ucuz birşeyiniz yok mu?	dahhah oojooz beershayeeneez yok moo
Fine, that will do.	İyi, şimdilik yeterli.	eeyee sheemdeeleek yehtehrlee

EATING OUT

If you enjoyed the wine, you may want to say:

Please bring me another...	**Bir ... daha getirin, lütfen.**	beer...dahhah gᵛehteereen lewtfehn
glass/carafe/bottle	**bardak/sürahi/şişe**	bahrdahk/sewrahhee/sheesheh
What's this wine called?	**Bu şarabın adı nedir?**	boo shahrahbın ahdı nehdeer
Where does this wine come from?	**Bu şarap nereden geliyor?**	boo shahrahp nehrehdehn gᵛehleeyor
How old is this wine?	**Bu şarap kaç seneliktir?**	boo shahrahp kahch sehnehleekteer

dry	**sek**	sehk
red	**kırmızı**	kırmızı
rosé	**pembe**	pehmbeh
sparkling	**köpüklü**	kurpewklew
sweet	**tatlı**	tahtlı
white	**beyaz**	behyahz
chilled	**buzlu**	boozloo
at room temperature	**oda ısısında**	odah ısıssındah

Other alcoholic drinks

You may want to order one of the following sometime during your trip, although you mustn't expect to find such a wide choice everywhere:

aperitif	**aperitif**	ahpehreeteef
beer	**bira**	beerah
bloody Mary	**bloody Mary (blodi Meri)**	blodee mehree
Bourbon	**Bourbon (Burbon)**	boorbon
gin	**cin**	jeen
gin-fizz	**cin-fiz**	jeen-feez
gin-tonic	**cin-tonik**	jeen-toneek
cider	**elma şarabı**	ehlmah shahrahbı
brandy, cognac	**konyak/kanyak**	konyahk/kahnyahk
liqueur	**likör**	leekurr
port	**porto**	porto
rum	**rum**	room

Scotch	Scotch (Skoç)	skoch
sherry	sherry (şeri)	shehree
vermouth	vermut	vehrmoot
whisky	viski	veeskee
neat (straight)	sek	sehk
on the rocks	buzlu	boozloo
whisky and soda	viski-soda	veeskee-sodah
vodka	votka	votkah
screwdriver	votka-portakal suyu	votkah-portahkahl sooyoo

glass	bardak*/kadeh**	bahrdahk/kahdehh
bottle	şişe	sheesheh
single (shot)	tek	tehk
double (double shot)	duble	doobleh

Rakı is without a doubt the national drink. This aniseed liqueur is usually drunk with the meal diluted with water which gives it a milky appearance. It's frequently referred to as lion's milk. You can also drink *rakı* neat (straight).

If you're really game, try a concoction popular amongst Turkish soldiers. It's made by mixing equal portions of *rakı* and beer. Four well-known brands of *rakı* are:

Altınbaş Rakısı	ahltınbahsh rahkıssı
Klüp Rakısı	klewprahkıssı
Tek Rakı	tehk rahkı
Yeni Rakı	yehnee rahkı

I'd like to try a glass of ..., please.	Bir ... istiyorum.	beer ... eesteeyoroom
Are there any local specialities?	Özel bir içkiniz var mı?	urzehl beer eechkeeneez vahr mı
Please bring me a ... of ...	Bana bir ... ... getirin lütfen.	bahnah beer ...... grehteereen lewtfehn

> **ŞEREFE !**
> (sherehfeh)
> **CHEERS !**

* for non-alcoholic drinks   ** for alcoholic drinks

Other beverages

You'll certainly want to try the world-renowned Turkish coffee which will probably be the only type of coffee you'll be able to find. Don't forget that Turkish coffee is quite strong but almost invariably well brewed. When the coffee is served—grounds and all—let it sit a minute so that the grounds can settle to the bottom of the cup, and then sip only half the cup. You'll have to let the waiter know in advance whether or not you want your coffee sweetened as the sugar and coffee are brewed together. Milk or cream isn't served with the coffee.

coffee without sugar	**sade kahve**	sahdeh kahhveh
slightly sweetened	**az şekerli kahve**	ahz shehkehrlee kahhveh
sweet	**orta şekerli kahve**	ortah shehkehrlee kahhveh
very sweet	**çok şekerli kahve**	chok shehkehrlee kahhveh

Another popular drink which goes well with a meal is *ayran* (igh**rahn**), yoghurt mixed with water and a pinch of salt.

I'd like a...	... istiyorum.	...eesteeyoroom
Have you any...?	... var mı?	... vahr mı
chocolate	**Çikolata**	cheekolahtah
coffee	**Kahve**	kahhveh
cup of coffee	**Bir fincan kahve**	beer feenjahn kahhveh
coffee with cream	**Sütlü kahve**	sewtlew kahhveh
fruit juice	**Meyve suyu**	mayveh sooyoo
grapefruit	**Greypfrut**	graypfroot
lemon/orange	**Limon/Portakal**	leemon/portahkahl
pineapple/tomato	**Ananas/Domates**	ahnahnahss/domahtehss
lemonade	**Limonata**	leemonahtah
milk	**Süt**	sewt
milkshake	**Frape**	frahpeh
mineral water	**Maden suyu**	mahdehn sooyoo
orangeade	**Portakal şurubu**	portahkahl shoorooboo
soda water	**Soda**	sodah
squash (soda pop)	**Meyveli gazoz**	mayvehlee gahzoz
tea	**Çay**	chahy
with milk/lemon	**Sütlü/Limonlu**	sewtlew/leemonloo
iced tea	**Buzlu çay**	boozloo chahy
tonic water	**Tonik**	toneek

Coffeehouse

The coffeehouse is an institution in Turkey. Usually rather modest establishments, they're ubiquitous in towns, and there's at least one coffeehouse in even the tiniest hamlet.

Like our pub or tavern, the coffeehouse is the exclusive gathering place of the men. Women are generally unwelcome but well-educated Turkish ladies and distaff Westerners might cross the threshold of the coffeehouse.

You'll see men sitting in groups vigorously discussing politics, the weather, football or otherwise solving the problems of the world over a glass of tea or a cup of strong coffee. Other customers will be concentrating on a game of backgammon or playing cards. You'll probably be stared at out of curiosity. And some Turks will doubtless want to strike up a friendly conversation with you.

Often great wreaths of smoke fill the coffeehouses as some men puff listlessly away on their *nargile* (water pipe). Should you want to try one just ask:

Can you prepare a water pipe for me?	**Bana bir nargile hazırlar mısınız, lütfen?**	bahnah beer nahrgeeleh hahzirlahr missiniz lewtfehn

For a small fee, the waiter will bring you a water pipe. Always smoke the water pipe in a small group, passing the mouthpiece around. Draw the smoke up very slowly. Even if you're a heavy smoker, the *nargile* may give you a mild feeling of euphoria.

More often than not, there'll be no food sold at a coffeehouse. Sometimes a vendor might pass through selling sesame rolls or pasties.

EATING OUT

Eating light—Snacks

I'll have one of those, please.	Şunlardan bir tane istiyorum, lütfen.	shoonlahrdahn beer tahneh eesteeyoroom lewtfehn
Give me two of those and one of those.	Bunlardan iki, bunlardan da bir tane verin.	boonlahrdahn eekee boonlahrdahn **dah** beer tahneh vehreen
to the left/to the right	solda/sağda	soldah/sahdah
above/below	üstünde/altında	ewstewndeh/ahltındah
Please give me a/an/some…	… verir misiniz?	… vehreer meesseeneez
biscuits (Br.)	Birkaç bisküvi	beerkahch beeskewvee
bread	Biraz ekmek	beerahz ehkmehk
butter	Tereyağı	tehrehyahı
cake	Bir pasta	beer pahstah
candy	Şekerleme	shehkehrlehmeh
chocolate (bar)	Bir parça çikolata	beer pahrchah cheekolahtah
cookies	Birkaç galeta	beerkahch gahlehtah
hamburger	Bir hamburger	beer hahmboorgʸehr
hot dog	Bir sosisli sandviç	beer sosseeslee sahndveech
ice-cream	Bir dondurma	beer dondoormah
pastry	Bir tatlı	beer tahtlı
pie	Bir börek	beer burrehk
roll	Birkaç küçük ekmek	beerkahch kewchewk ehkmehk
salad	Biraz salata	beerahz sahlahtah
sandwich	Bir sandviç	beer sahndveech
sweets	Birkaç bonbon	beerkahch bonbon
toast	Bir tost	beer tost
How much is that?	Bu ne kadar?	boo neh kahdahr

Travelling around

Plane

This section is very brief because at any airport or airline office you're sure to find someone who speaks English.

Do you speak English?	İngilizce biliyor musunuz?	eeng°eeleezjeh beeleeyor moossoonooz
Is there a flight to Antalya?	Antalya'ya uçuş var mı?	ahntahlyah yah oochoosh vahr mı
Is it a nonstop flight?	Bu bir direkt uçuş mudur?	boo beer deerehkt oochoosh moodoor
Do I have to change planes?	Uçak değiştirmem lâzım mı?	oochahk deheeshteermehm larzım mı
Can I make a connection to Adana?	Adana için bir aktarma yapabilir miyim?	ahdahnah eecheen beer ahktahrmah yahpahbeeleer meeyeem
I'd like a ticket to Samsun.	Samsun'a bir bilet istiyorum.	sahmsoonah beer beeleht eesteeyoroom
What's the fare to Trabzon?	Trabzon'a bir biletin fiatı ne kadardır?	trahbzonah beer beelehteen feeahtı neh kahdahrdır
single (one-way)	gidiş	g°eedeesh
return (roundtrip)	gidiş-dönüş	g°eedeesh-durnewsh
What time does the plane take off?	Uçak saat kaçta kalkar?	oochahk saht kahchtah kahlkahr
What time do I have to check in?	Bagajların kaydını saat kaçta yaptırmalıyım?	bahgahzhlahrın kahydını saht kahchtah yahptırmahlıyım
What's the flight number?	Uçuş numarası kaçtır?	oochoosh noomahrahssı kahchtır
What time do we arrive?	Sat kaçta varırız?	saht kahchtah vahrırız

VARIŞ ARRIVAL	DEPARTURE **ÇIKIŞ**

Train and bus

With the exception of the Istanbul–Ankara line, the national railway network can only be described as somewhat less than adequate.

There are first- and second-class compartments—and sometimes even third class. All long-distance trains have sleeping- and dining-cars. Comfort is minimal except on select trains.

There are three major types of trains:

motortren (motortrehn)	a local train stopping at all stations
ekspres (ehksprehss)	an express train stopping only at principal stations
yolcu treni (yoljoo trehnee)	a long-distance train stopping at all stations

In Turkey, travel by bus may be preferable to rail. There are many private bus companies operating frequent services to cities and out-of-the-way villages throughout the country. The fare—always cheap—varies according to the class of bus.

In some cases you may find yourself riding in a wheezing pre-war-model bus with numerous villagers accompanied by their chickens and goats. Such a bus can be flagged down along the route.

A better, more comfortable class of bus is still a bargain and may even be a modern, air-conditioned vehicle. For these buses you'll buy a ticket in advance at the town's main terminal where all the bus companies are represented. Frequently you may reserve your seat ahead of time. You may have piped-in music and an attendant who'll come around and sprinkle cologne over your hands as the bus bumps along over the dusty roads. Some buses make night runs.

Phrases in this section can easily be adapted to either bus or train travel.

To the railway station

Where's the railway station?	İstasyon nerededir?	eestahssyon nehrehdehdeer
Where's the bus station?	Otobüs durağı nerededir?	otobewss doorarı nehrehdehdeer
Taxi, please!	Taksi!	tahksee
Take me to the railway station.	Beni istasyona götürün.	behnee eestahssyonah gurtewrewn
What's the fare?	Ücret ne tutar?	ewjreht neh tootahr

KAMBİYO	CURRENCY EXCHANGE

Where's the...?

Where is/are the...	... nerededir?	... nehrehdehdeer
barber's	Berber dükkânı	behrbehr dewkarnı
booking office	Rezervasyon bürosu	rehzehrvahssyon bewrossoo
buffet	Büfe	bewfeh
currency exchange office	Kambiyo bürosu	kahmbeeyo bewrossoo
information office	Danışma bürosu	dahnıshmah bewrossoo
left luggage office (baggage check)	Emânet	ehmahneht
lost-property (lost and found) office	Kayıp eşyalar bürosu	kahyıp ehshyahlahr bewrossoo
luggage lockers	Emânet kasası	ehmahneht kahssahssı
news-stand	Gazete bayii	gahzehteh bahyee
platform 7	Peron 7	pehron 7
reservations office	Rezervasyon bürosu	rehzehrvahssyon bewrossoo
restaurant	Lokanta	lokahntah
ticket office	Bilet gişesi	beeleht gʸeeshehssee
waiting-room	Bekleme salonu	behklehmeh sahlonoo
Where are the toilets?	Tuvaletler nerededir?	toovahlehtlehr nehrehdehdeer

TRAVELLING AROUND

FOR TAXI, see page 27

Inquiries

In Turkey **i** means information office.

When is the... train/bus to Eskisehir?	Eskişehir'e ... tren/otobüs ne zaman?	ehskeeshehheereh ... trehn/otobewss neh zahmahn
first/last/next	ilk/son/gelecek	eelk/son/gᵛehlehjehk
What time does the train for Balikesir leave?	Balıkesir treni saat kaçta hareket ediyor?	bahlıkehsseer trehnee saht kahchtah hahrehkeht ehdeeyor
What's the fare to Erzurum?	Erzurum için ücret nedir?	ehrzooroom eecheen ewjreht nehdeer
Is it a through train?	Bu tren ekspres midir?	boo trehn ehksprehss meedeer
Will the train leave on time?	Tren zamanında kalkar mı?	trehn zahmahnındah kahlkahr mı
What time does the train arrive at Manisa?	Tren Manisa'ya saat kaçta varıyor?	trehn mahneessahyah saht kahchtah vahrıyor
Is there a dining-car on the train?	Trende yemekli vagon var mı?	trehndeh yehmehklee vahgon vahr mı
Is there a sleeping-car on the train?	Trende yataklı vagon var mı?	trehndeh yahtahklı vahgon vahr mı
Does the train stop at Yesilyurt?	Tren Yeşilyurt'da durur mu?	trehn yehsheelyoort'dah dooroor moo
What platform does the train for Aydin leave from?	Aydın treni hangi perondan kalkıyor?	ahydın trehnee hahngᵛee pehrondahn kahlkıyor
What platform does the train from ... arrive at?	... treni hangi perona giriyor?	... trehnee hahngᵛee pehronah gᵛeereeyor

GIRIŞ	ENTRANCE
ÇIKIŞ	EXIT
PERONLARA GİDER	TO THE PLATFORMS

TRAVELLING AROUND

Bu tren ekspresdir.	It's a through train.
...'de aktarma yapmanız lâzım.	You have to change at...
...'de aktarma yapın ve banliyöye binin.	Change at ... and get a local train.
... peron ...dır.	Platform...is...
orada/yukarıda solda/sağda	over there/upstairs on the left/on the right
...'a saat ...da tren var.	There's a train to ... at ...
Treniniz ... perondan kalkacak.	Your train will leave from platform...
... dakikalık bir gecikme olacak.	There'll be a delay of... minutes.

Tickets

want a ticket to Bandirma.	Bandırma'ya bir bilet istiyorum.	bahndırmahyah beer beeleht eesteeyoroom
single (one-way)	gidiş	g^yeedeesh
return (roundtrip)	gidiş-dönüş	g^yeedeesh-durnewsh
first class	birinci sınıf	beereenjee sınıf
sn't it half price or the boy/girl?	Çocuk için yarım tarife değil mi?	chojook eecheen yahrım tahreefeh deheel mee
He's/She's 13.	13 yaşındadır.	13 yahshındahdır

Birinci mevki mi, ikinci mevki mi?	First or second class?
Gidiş mi, gidiş-dönüş mü?	Single or return (one-way or roundtrip)?
Kaç yaşındadır?	How old is he/she?

All aboard...

Is this the right platform for the train to Ankara?	Ankara treni için doğru peronda mıyız?	ahnkahrah trehnee eecheen doroo pehrondah mıyız
Is this the right train to Mersin?	Mersin treni bu mudur?	mehrseen trehnee boo moodoor
Excuse me. May I get by?	Affedersiniz, geçebilir miyim?	ahffehdehrseeneez g'ehchehbeeleer meeyeer
Is this seat taken?	Bu yerin sahibi var mı?	boo yehreen sahheebee vahr mı

SİGARA İÇİLMEZ
NO SMOKING

I think that's my seat.	Zannedersem burası benim yerim.	zahnnehdehrsehm boorahsı behneem yehreem
Would you let me know before we get to Izmir?	İzmir'e varırken bana haber verir misiniz?	eezmeereh vahrırkehn bahnah hahbehr vehreer meesseeneez
What station is this?	Bu hangi istasyon, acaba?	boo hahng'ree eestahssyon ahjahbah
How long does the train stop here?	Tren burada ne kadar durur?	trehn boorahdah neh kahdahr dooroor
When do we get to Denizli?	Denizli'ye ne zaman varıyoruz?	dehneezleeyeh neh zahmahn vahrıyorooz

Sometime on the journey the ticket collector (*kondüktör—* kon**dewk**turr) will come around and say: *Biletler lütfen!* (Tickets, please).

Eating

Long-distance trains have dining-cars serving both full meals and snacks. Buses make meal-time stops at roadside inns or in small villages.

If you want a full meal in the dining-car, you may have to get a ticket from the steward who'll come round to your compartment.

| First/Second call for dinner. | **Yemek için birinci/ ikinci çağrı.** | yehmehk eecheen beereeenjee/ eekeenjee charrı |
| Where's the dining-car? | **Yemekli vagon nerededir?** | yehmehklee vahgon nehrehdehdeer |

Sleeping

Are there any free compartments in the sleeping-car?	**Yataklı vagonda boş kompartman var mı?**	yahtahklı vahgondah bosh kompahrtımahn vahr mı
Where's the sleeping-car?	**Yataklı vagon nerededir?**	yahtahklı vahgon nehrehdehdeer
Where's my berth?	**Kuşetim hangisi acaba?**	kooshehteem hahng'eessee ahjahbah
Compartments 18 and 19, please.	**18. ve 19. kompart-manlar, lütfen.**	18. veh 19. kompahrt-mahnlahr lewtfehn
'd like a lower berth.	**Altta bir kuşet tercih ederim.**	ahlttah beer koosheht tehrjeehh ehdehreem
Would you make up our berths?	**Kuşetlerimizi hazırlar mısınız?**	kooshehtlehreemeezee hahzırlahr mıssınız
Would you call me at 7 o'clock?	**Beni saat 7 de kaldırır mısınız?**	behnee saht 7 deh kahldırır mıssınız
Would you bring me some coffee in the morning?	**Sabah bana kahve getirir misiniz?**	sahbahh bahnah kahhveh gehteereer meesseeneez

Baggage and porters

| Can you help me with my bags? | **Çantalarımı taşımama yardım eder misiniz?** | chahntahlahrımı tahshımahmah yahrdım ehdehr meesseeneez |
| Please put them down here. | **Lütfen buraya bırakın.** | lewtfehn boorahyah bırahkın |

FOR PORTERS, see also page 24

TRAVELLING AROUND

Lost!

We hope you'll have no need for the following phrases on your trip...but just in case:

Where's the lost-property (lost and found) office?	**Kayıp eşyalar bürosu nerededir?**	kahyıp ehshyahlahr bewrossoo nehrehdehdeer
I've lost my...	**... mı kaybettim.**	... mı kahybehtteem
this morning	**bu sabah**	boo sahbahh
yesterday	**dün**	dewn
I lost it in...	**Onu ...da kaybettim.**	onoo ...dah kahybehtteem
It's very valuable.	**Çok değerlidir.**	chok dehehrleedeer

Time-tables

If you intend to do a lot of rail travel, it might be a good idea to buy a time-table. These are based on the 24-hour clock and are on sale at ticket and inquiry offices and in some bookshops.

I'd like to buy a time-table.	**Bir tarife almak istiyorum.**	beer tahreefeh ahlmahk eesteeyoroom

Bus

You pay your fare when you get on the bus. In major cities it may be worthwhile to get a runabout ticket (which allows unlimited travel during a fixed period) or a booklet of tickets.

I'd like a booklet of tickets.	**Bir bilet karnesi istiyorum.**	beer beeleht kahrnehssee eesteeyoroom
Where can I get a bus to Topkapi?	**Topkapı sarayına otobüs nereden kalkar?**	topkahpı sahrahyınah otobewss nehrehdehn kahlkahr

What bus do I take for Taksim?	Taksim'e gitmek için hangi otobüse binmeliyim?	tahkseemeh g^yeetmehk eecheen hahng^yee otobewsseh beenmehleeyeem
Where's the...?	... nerededir?	... nehrehdehdeer
bus stop	Otobüs durağı	otobewss doorahı
terminus	Son durak	son doorahk
When is the ... bus to Emirgan?	Emirgân'a ... otobüs ne zaman?	ehmeergarnah ... otobewss neh zahmahn
first/last/next	ilk/son/gelecek	eelk / son / g^yehlehjehk
How often do the buses leave for Bostanci?	Bostancı'ya ne kadar zamanda bir otobüs vardır?	bostahnjıyah neh kahdahr zahmahndah beer otobewss vahrdır
How much is the fare to...?	...'a ücret nedir?	...ah ewjreht nehdeer
Do I have to change buses?	Aktarma yapman gerekir mi?	ahktahrmah yahpmahm g^yehrehkeer mee
How long does the journey take?	Yolculuk ne kadar sürer?	yoljoolook neh kahdahr sewrehr
Will you tell me when to get off?	Ne zaman inmen gerektiğini söyler misiniz?	neh zahmahn eenmehm g^yehrehkteenee surlehr meesseeneez
I want to get off at Florya.	Florya'da inmek istiyorum.	floryahdah eenmehk eesteeyoroom
Please let me off at the next stop.	Beni gelecek durakta indirin, lütfen.	behnee g^yehlehjehk doorahktah eendeereen lewtfehn
May I please have my luggage?	Bagajımı verir misiniz?	bahgahzhımı vehreer meesseeneez

OTOBÜS	REGULAR BUS STOP
İHTİYÂRİ DURAK	STOPS ON REQUEST

Going by boat

Travelling by boat can be a pleasant and economical way of getting around. There are regular services along the Aegan, Black Sea and Mediterranean coasts as well as across the Marmara Sea where you can make stops at the Prince Islands. Boats also serve the fabled Golden Horn and the Bosphorus. There may be one or several categories of fares.

There are frequent ferry-boat services across the Bosphorus and the Marmara Sea, linking Turkey in Europe with Anatolia. Though you may choose to enter Asia by crossing the newly constructed bridge which straddles the Bosphorus strait it's hard to match the bustling atmosphere around the dock and the thrill of Turkish Asia looming up before you.

| When does the next ferry-boat leave for Üsküdar? | Üsküdar'a gelecek araba vapuru ne zaman kalkıyor? | ewskewdahrah gᵛehlehjehk ahrahbah vahpooroo neh zahmahn kahlkıyor |
| How much do I have to pay for the car? | Otomobil için ne kadar ödemem lâzım? | otomobeel eecheen neh kahdahr urdehmehm larzım |

Other means of transport

bicycle	bisiklet	beesseekleht
boat	sandal	sahndahl
houseboat	yüzerev	yewzehrehv
motorboat	deniz motoru	dehneez motoroo
rowing-boat	kayık	kahyık
sailing-boat	yelkenli	yehlkehnlee
helicopter	helikopter	hehleekoptehr
hitch-hiking	oto-stop	oto-stop
horseback riding	ata binme	ahtah beenmeh
moped (motor-bike)	motorlu bisiklet	motorloo beesseekleht
motorcycle	motosiklet	motosseekleht

and if you're really stuck, go...

| walking | yürüyün | yewrewyewn |

Around and about—Sightseeing

Here we're more concerned with the cultural aspect of life than with entertainment and, for the moment, with towns rather than the countryside. If you want a guide book, ask…

Can you recommend a good guide book for…?	… için iyi bir rehber kitabı tavsiye edebilir misiniz?	… eecheen eeyee beer rehhbehr keetahbı tahvseeyeh ehdehbeeleer meesseeneez
Is there a tourist office?	Turist bürosu var mıdır?	tooreest bewrosso vahr mıdır
Where's the tourist office/information centre?	Turist bürosu/ danışma merkezi nerededir?	tooreest bewrossoo/ dahnıshmah mehrkehzee nehrehdehdeer
What are the main points of interest?	En ilginç şeyler nelerdir?	ehn eelgʸeench shaylehr nehlehrdeer
We're here for…	… buradayız.	… boorahdahyız
only a few hours	Sadece birkaç saatliğine	sahdehjeh beerkahch sahtleeneh
a day	Bir günlüğüne	beer gʸewnlewneh
three days	Üç günlüğüne	ewch gʸewnlewneh
a week	Bir haftalığına	beer hahftahlınah
Can you recommend a sightseeing tour?	Bir şehir turu tavsiye edebilir misiniz?	beer shehheer tooroo tahvseeyeh ehdehbeeleer meesseeneez
Where does the bus start from?	Otobüs nereden kalkar?	otobewss nehrehdehn kahlkahr
Will it pick us up at the hotel?	Bizi otelden alacak mı?	beezee otehldehn ahlahjahk mı
What bus do we take?	Hangi otobüse bineceğiz?	hahngʸee otobewsseh beenehjeheez
How much does the tour cost?	Tur ne kadar tutar?	toor neh kahdahr tootahr
What time does the tour start?	Tur saat kaçta başlar?	toor saht kahchtah bahshlahr
We'd like to rent a car for the day.	Bir günlüğüne bir otomobil kiralamak istiyoruz.	beer gewnlewneh beer otomobeel keerahlahmahk eesteeyoroom

FOR TIME OF DAY, see page 178

SIGHTSEEING

Is there an English-speaking guide?	İngilizce bilen bir rehber var mı?	eeng'eeleezjeh beelehn beer rehhbehr vahr mı
Where is/Where are the…?	… nerededir?	… nehrehdehdeer
aquarium	Akvaryum	ahkvahryoom
art gallery	Sanat galerisi	sahnaht gahlehreessee
building	Büyük bina	bewyewk beenah
business district	İş yeri	eesh yehree
castle	Şato	shahto
catacombs	Katakomb	kahtahkomb
cathedral	Katedral	kahtehdrahl
cave	Mağara	mahrah
cemetery	Mezarlık	mehzahrlık
city centre	Şehir merkezi	shehheer mehrkehzee
city hall	Belediye sarayı	behlehdeeyeh sahrahyı
church	Kilise	keeleesseh
concert hall	Konser salonu	konsehr sahlonoo
court house	Adliye	ahdleeyeh
docks	Rıhtım	rıhhtım
downtown area	Şehir merkezi	shehheer mehrkehzee
exhibition	Sergi	sehrg'ee
factory	Fabrika	fahbreekah
fortress	Kale	kahleh
fountain	Çeşme	cheshmeh
gardens	Bahçe	bahhcheh
harbour	Liman	leemahn
lake	Göl	gurl
library	Kütüphane	kewtewphahneh
market	Çarşı	chahrshı
memorial	Anıt	ahnıt
monastery	Manastır	mahnahstır
monument	Âbide	arbeedeh
mosque	Câmi	jahmee
museum	Müze	mewzeh
observatory	Rasathane	rahssahthahneh
old city	Eski şehir	ehskee shehheer
opera house	Opera	opehrah
palace	Saray	sahrahy
park	Park	pahrk
parliament building	Parlamento binası	pahrlahmehnto beenahssı
planetarium	Rasathane	rahssahthahneh
presidential palace	Cumhurbaşkanlığı köşkü	joomhoorbahshkahnlı kurshkew
royal palace	Kraliyet sarayı	krahleeyeht sahrahyı
ruins	Harabeler	hahrahbehlehr

hopping centre	Alışveriş merkezi	ahlıshvehreesh mehrkehzee
tadium	Stadyom	stahdyom
tatue	Heykel	haykehl
tock exchange	Borsa	borsah
upreme court	Yargıtay	yahrgıtahy
ynagogue	Sinagog	seenahgog
elevision studios	Televizyon stüdyosu	tehlehveezyon stewdyossoo
emple	Tapınak	tahpınahk
omb	Mezar	mehzahr
ower	Kule	kooleh
niversity	Universite	ewneevehrseeteh
aults	Kemerler	kehmehrlehr
oo	Hayvanat bahçesi	hahyvahnaht bahhchehssee

Admission

s ... open on Sundays?	... pazar günleri açık mıdır?	... pahzahr gewnlehree ahchık mıdır
When does it pen/close?	Ne zaman açılır/kapanır?	neh zahmahn ahchılır/kahpahnır
low much is the ntrance fee?	Giriş ücreti nedir?	gᵛeereesh ewjrehtee nehdeer
s there any eduction for...?	... için indirim var mı?	... eecheen eendeereem vahr mı
tudents/children	Öğrenciler/Çocuklar	urrehnjeelehr/chojooklahr
lere's my ticket.	İşte biletim.	eeshteh beelehteem
lere are our ckets.	İşte biletlerimiz.	eeshteh beelehtlehreemeez
lave you a guide ook (in English)?	(İngilizce) rehber kitabınız var mı?	(eengᵛeeleezjeh) rehhbehr keetahbınız vahr mı
an I buy a atalogue?	Bir katalog satın alabilir miyim?	beer kahtahlog sahtın ahlahbeeleer meeyeem
s it all right to ake pictures?	Fotoğraf çekilebilir mi?	fotorahf chehkehlehbeeleer mee

GİRİŞ ÜCRETSİZDİR	ADMISSION FREE
FOTOĞRAF ÇEKMEK YASAKTIR	NO CAMERAS ALLOWED

SIGHTSEEING

Who—What—When?

What's that building?	**Bu bina nedir?**	boo beenah nehdeer
Who was the...?	**Bunun ...ı kimdir?**	boonoon ...ı keemdeer
architect	**mimar**	meemahr
artist	**sanatkâr**	sahnahtkarr
painter	**ressam**	rehssahm
sculptor	**heykeltraş**	haykehltrahsh
Who built it?	**Kim inşa ettirmiştir?**	keem eenshah ehtteermeeshteer
Who painted that picture?	**Bu tabloyu kim yapmıştır?**	boo tahbloyoo keem yahpmıshtır
When did he live?	**Hangi devirde yaşamıştır?**	hahngᵛee dehveerdeh yahshahmıshtır
When was it built?	**Ne zaman inşa edilmiştir?**	neh zahmahn eenshah ehdeelmeeshteer
Where's the house where... lived?	**...'n yaşadığı ev nerededir?**	...n yahshahdı ehv nehrehdehdeer
We're interested in...	**... ile ilgileniyoruz.**	... eeleh eelgᵛeelehneeyorooz
antiques	**Antika eşya**	ahnteekah ehshyah
archaeology	**Arkeoloji**	ahrkeholozhee
art	**Sanat**	sahnaht
botany	**Botanik**	botahneek
ceramics	**Seramik**	sehrahmeek
coins	**Madenî para**	mahdehnee pahrah
crafts	**El sanatları**	ehl sahnahtlahrı
fine arts	**Güzel sanatlar**	gewzehl sahnahtlahr
furniture	**Mobilya**	mobeelyah
geology	**Jeoloji**	zheholozhee
history	**Tarih**	tahreehh
medicine	**Tıp**	tıp
music	**Müzik**	mewzeek
natural history	**Tabiat bilgisi**	tahbeeaht beelgᵛeessee
ornithology	**Ornitoloji**	orneetolozhee
painting	**Resim**	rehsseem
pottery	**Çömlekçilik**	churmlehkcheeleek
prehistory	**Tarih öncesi**	tahreehh urnjehssee
sculpture	**Heykelcilik**	haykehljeeleek
zoology	**Zooloji**	zoolozhee
Where's the... department?	**... kısmı nerededir?**	... kısmı nehrehdehdeer

Just the adjective you've been looking for...

It's...

amazing	**Şaşırtıcı.**	shah**shır**tıjı
awful	**Korkunç.**	kor**koonch**
beautiful	**Güzel.**	ge**wzehl**
gloomy	**Kasvetli.**	kahs**veht**lee
impressive	**Etkileyici.**	ehtkeelehyeejee
interesting	**İlginç.**	eelg**reench**
magnificent	**Harikulâde.**	hahreekoolardeh
monumental	**Heybetli.**	hay**beht**lee
overwhelming	**Çok etkileyici.**	chok ehtkeelehyeejee
sinister	**Uğursuz.**	oor**sooz**
strange	**Tuhaf.**	too**hahf**
superb	**Muhteşem.**	moohh**teh**shehm
terrible	**Dehşetli.**	dehh**sheht**lee
terrifying	**Dehşet verici.**	dehh**sheht** vehreejee
tremendous	**Heybetli.**	hav**beht**lee
ugly	**Çirkin.**	cheer**keen**

Mosques and religious services

Turkey is a Moslem country, and you'll certainly want to take the opportunity of visiting some of the nation's historic and impressive mosques.

After the inspiring minarets and cupolas—landmarks visible from afar—have drawn you almost irresistibly towards them, you'll find the interior decor equally entrancing. Delicately engraved ceramic tiles bearing inscriptions in Arabic and Persian script decorate the walls, and the columns and arches are often richly carved.

If these magnificent interiors tempt you to get out your camera you must first ask permission to take photographs, and even then you'll have to be extremely discreet about it during prayer time.

Despite the secular orientation of the state since the days of Atatürk, the Moslem call to prayer still take precedence over most other activities and the mosques at this hour are crowded with the faithful. The sexes are strictly separated in the mosque, the women demurely occupying the rear section of the building where they will not be a distraction to their menfolk during worship.

Though visitors of obviously foreign aspect will be allowed somewhat more latitude in their observance of Moslem manners, there are certain rules that you must respect. First, you'll have to remove your shoes at the entrance to the mosque and either go barefoot or don a pair of the oversized slippers which are provided for visitors' use. Your dress must be traditionally decent (no shorts or miniskirts!) and you should not walk in front of people who are in prayer. A final point of importance is that women are not allowed to wander at will around the mosque. Though these restrictions may irk a little you'll find that their observance will avoid possible unpleasantness and earn you a good deal of respect.

As to churches and synagogues, these are to be found only in the country's major cities. Services are often held in English. For details, inquire at the local tourist office.

Is there a…near here?	Yakınlarda bir … var mıdır?	yahkınlahrdah beer… vahr mıdır
Catholic church	Katolik kilisesi	kahtoleek keeleessehssee
Mosque	câmi	jahmee
Orthodox church	Ortodoks kilisesi	ortodoks keeleessehssee
Protestant church	Protestan kilisesi	protehstahn keeleessehssee
Synagogue	sinagog	seenahgog
At what time is…?	… saat kaçtadır?	… saht kachtahdır
mass	Âyin	aryeen
divine liturgy	Kutsal âyin	kootsahl aryeen
the service	Âyin	aryeen
Where can I find a… who speaks English?	İngilizce bilen bir … nerede bulabilirim?	eengˀeeleezjeh beelehn beer … nehrehdeh boolahbeeleereem
priest	katolik (ortodoks) rahip	kahtoleek (ortodoks) rahheep
minister	protestan vâiz	protehstahn vaheez
rabbi	haham	hahhahm

Relaxing

Cinema (movies)—Theatre

Since cinema showings are seldom continuous, you can buy your tickets in advance. Most foreign films are shown in their original language. There are also locally-produced films. You can expect one feature film, a newsreel, perhaps a short documentary and numerous commercials.

Among the most popular forms of classical entertainment are the *Karagöz* and *Hacivat* shadow plays—a sort of a Turkish Punch and Judy show. The two "heros", *Karagöz* and *Hacivat,* are good friends but are continually scrapping with one another. Though he has had little schooling, *Hacivat* considers himself a clever fellow. *Karagöz,* on the other hand, has never been to school. Their patter and discussions are comical and satirical. Even if you don't understand a word of Turkish, you'll enjoy the animated antics of the characters and the lively response of the audience.

In addition, especially during the theatre season from October to May, you'll be able to attend plays, the opera, concerts or ballets. Art forms—both Western and Near Eastern—range from ancient to modern works.

You can find out what's playing from newspapers and posters.

Where can I see a shadow play?	**Nerede bir gölge oyunu görebilirim?**	nehrehdeh beer gurlgeh oyoonoo gurrehbeeleereem
What's showing at the cinema tonight?	**Bu akşam sinemada ne oynuyor?**	boo ahkshahm seenehmahdah neh oynooyor
What's playing at the... theatre?	**... tiyatrosunda ne oynuyor?**	...teeyahtrossoondah neh oynooyor
What sort of play is it?	**Ne tür bir oyundur?**	neh tewr beer oyoondoor
Who's it by?	**Kimin eseridir?**	keemeen ehssehreedeer

Can you recommend a...?	... tavsiye edebilir misiniz?	...tahvseeyeh ehdehbeeleer meesseeneez
good film	İyi bir film	eeyee beer feeleem
comedy	Bir komedi	beer komehdee
drama	Bir dram	beer drahm
musical	Bir müzikal oyun	beer mewzeekahl oyoon
revue	Bir rövü	beer rehvew
thriller	Heyecanlı bir filim	hehyehjahnlı beer feeleem
Western	Bir kovboy filmi	beer kovboy feelmee

At what theatre is that new play by... being performed?	...'nın yeni oyunu hangi tiyatroda oynanıyor?	...nın yehnee oyoonoo hahngvee teeyahtrodah oynahnıyor
Where's that new film by... being shown?	...'nın yeni filmi nerede oynuyor?	...nın yehnee feelmee nehrehdeh oynooyor
Who's in it?	Kimler oynuyor?	keemlehr oynooyor
Who's the director?	Rejisörü kim?	rehzheessurrew keem
What time does it begin?	Saat kaçta başlar?	sart kachtah bahshlahr
What time does it end?	Saat kaçta sona erer?	sart kachtah sonah ehrehr
What time does the first evening performance start?	İlk akşam seansı saat kaçta başlar?	eelk ahkshahm sehahnsı sart kachtah bahshlahr
Are there any tickets for tonight?	Bu akşam için bilet var mı?	boo ahkshahm eecheen beeleht vahr mı
How much are the tickets?	Biletler kaçadır?	beelehtlehr kahchahdır
I want to reserve two tickets for the show on Friday evening.	Cuma akşamı için iki yer ayırtmak istiyorum.	joomah ahkshahmı eecheen eekee yehr ahyırtmahk eesteeyoroom
Can I have a ticket for the matinée on Tuesday?	Perşembe günkü matine için bir bilet istiyorum?	pehrshehmbeh gewnkew mahteeneh eecheen beer beeleht eesteeyoroom
I want a seat in the stalls (orchestra).	Ön sıralarda bir yer istiyorum.	urn sırahlahrdah beer yehr eesteeyoroom
Not too far back.	Çok gerilerde olmasın.	chok gvehreelehrdeh olmahssın
Somewhere in the middle.	Ortalarda bir yerde.	ortahlahrdah beer yehrdeh

How much are the seats in the circle (mezzanine)?	**Üst balkon biletlerinin fiatı nedir?**	ewst bahl**kon** beelehtlehreeneen feeyahtı neh**deer**
May I please have a programme?	**Bir program verir misiniz?**	beer prograhm veh**reer** mees**seen**eez
Can I check this coat?	**Paltomu bırakabilir miyim?**	pahltomoo bırahkahbee**leer** mee**yeem**

Üzgünüm, bilet kalmadı.	I'm sorry, we're sold out.
Sadece üst balkonun sol tarafında birkaç yer kaldı.	There are only a few seats left in the circle (mezzanine).
Biletinizi görebilir miyim?	May I see your ticket?
Yeriniz burası.	This is your seat.

Opera—Ballet—Concert

Where's the opera house?	**Opera nerededir?**	opeh**rah** nehrehdeh**deer**
Where's the concert hall?	**Konser salonu nerededir?**	kon**sehr** sahlonoo nehrehdeh**deer**
What's on at the opera tonight?	**Operada bu akşam ne var?**	opehrah**dah** boo ahk**shahm** neh **vahr**
Who's singing?	**Kim söylüyor?**	keem surlew**yor**
What time does the programme start?	**Program saat kaçta başlıyor?**	pro**grahm** sart kahch**tah** bahsh**lıyor**
What orchestra is playing?	**Hangi orkestra çalıyor?**	hahng**ree** or**kehs**trah chah**lıyor**
What are they playing?	**Hangi eserleri çalıyorlar?**	hahng**ree** ehssehrleh**ree** chah**lıyorlahr**
Who's the conductor?	**Orkestra şefi kimdir?**	or**kehs**trah sheh**fee** keem**deer**

FOR TIPPING, see inside back-cover

RELAXING

Night-clubs

Night-clubs are pretty much the same the world over—particularly when it comes to inflated prices. You can expect to pay a cover charge. Your drinks will be expensive.

There are some reasonably priced places that provide good entertainment, so ask around. For a real Turkish-style night-club, try a *gazino,* a type of supper club for the family where you'll be entertained with Turkish music and dances. But find out the prices before you order—and allow for the various surcharges.

For most night-clubs a dark suit is sufficient.

Can you recommend a good night-club?	İyi bir gece klübü tavsiye edebilir misiniz?	eeyee beer gᵛehjeh klewbew tahvseeyeh ehdehbeeleer meesseeneez
Is there a floor show?	Bir şov var mıdır?	beer shov vahr mıdır
What time does the floor show start?	Şov saat kaçta başlar?	shov saht kachtah bahshlahr
Is evening dress necessary?	Gece kıyafeti mecbûri midir?	gᵛehjeh kıyahfehtee mehjbooree meedeer

And once inside...

A table for 2, please.	2 kişilik bir masa, lütfen.	2 keesheeleek beer mahssah lewtfehn
My name's...I reserved a table for 4.	Adım ...'dır, 4 kişilik bir masa ayırtmıştım.	ahdım ...dır 4 keesheeleek beer mahssah ahyırtmıshtım
I telephoned you earlier.	Size daha önce telefon etmiştim.	seezeh dahhah urnjeh tehlehfon ehtmeeshteem
We haven't got a reservation.	Sizin için rezervasyon yapılmamış.	seezeen eecheen rehzehrvahssyon yahpılmahmısh

RELAXING

Dancing

Where can we go dancing?	**Dans etmeye nereye gidebiliriz?**	dahnss ehtmehyeh nehrehyeh gᵛeedehbeeleereez
Is there a discotheque in town?	**Şehirde diskotek var mı?**	shehheerdeh deeskotehk vahr mı
There's a dance at the...	**...de dans var.**	...deh dahnss **vahr**
Would you like to dance?	**Dans eder misiniz?**	dahnss ehdehr meesseeneez
May I have this dance?	**Bu dansı bana lütfeder misiniz?**	boo dahnsı bahnah lewtfehdehr meesseeneez

Do you happen to play...?

On a rainy day, this page may solve your problems.

Do you happen to play chess/ backgammon?	**Satranç/tavla oynar mısınız?**	sahtranch/tahvlah oynahr mıssınız
I'm afraid I don't.	**Maalesef hayır.**	mahlehssehf hahyır
No, but I'll give you a game of draughts (checkers).	**Hayır, fakat isterseniz bir dama partisi yapabiliriz.**	hahyır fahkaht eestehrsehneez beer dahmah pahrteessee yahpahbeeleereez
king	**şah**	shahh
queen	**vezir**	vehzeer
castle (rook)	**kale**	kahleh
bishop	**fil**	feel
knight	**at**	aht
pawn	**piyon**	peeyon
check mate	**şah ve mat**	shahh veh maht
Do you play cards?	**Kâğıt oynar mısınız?**	kart oynahr mıssınız
bridge	**briç**	breech
canasta	**kanasta**	kahnahstah
gin rummy	**remi**	rehmee
pontoon (21)	**yirmibir**	yeermeebeer
poker	**poker**	pokehr

ace	**as**	ahss
king	**papaz**	pahpahz
queen	**kız**	kız
jack	**vale**	vahleh
joker	**joker**	zhokehr
hearts	**kupa**	koopah
diamonds	**karo**	kahro
clubs	**sinek**	seenehk
spades	**maça**	mahchah

Casino and gambling

The only Western-type casino in Turkey is the one in Istanbul at the Hilton Hotel. It's open from 8 p.m. till the wee hours of the morning. You'll need your passport to get in, and you must be over 21. This casino has most of the usual games including blackjack, craps, poker, roulette and slot machines.

You're likely to see an enthusiastic sidewalk shell game or similar forms of surreptitious gambling going on. But avoid these like the plague as they're nothing but con games designed to swindle you.

Sports

Some visitors to Turkey will want to attend the classic wrestling match where wrestlers weighing in at over 200 pounds rub olive oil over their bodies. Wrestling matches of this type are held annually at Kirkpinar in northwestern Thrace.

Football (soccer) is the country's most popular sport. At one time it was considered only a big-city sport but now you can attend an amateur game in many outlying areas.

Where's the nearest golf course?	**En yakın golf sahası nerededir?**	ehn yahkın golf sahhahssı nehrehdehdeer
Can we hire (rent) clubs?	**Golf sopası kiralıyabilir miyiz?**	golf sopahssı keerahlı-yahbeeleer meeyeez
Where are the tennis courts?	**Tenis kortları nerededir?**	tehneess kortlahrı nehrehdehdeer

RELAXING

Can I hire rackets?	**Raket kiralıyabilir miyim?**	rahkeht keerahlıyahbeeleer meeyeem
What's the charge per...?	**... ne kadardır?**	... neh kahdahrdır
day/round/hour	**Günlüğü/Partisi/ Saati**	gewnlew/pahrteessee/ sartee
Where's the nearest race course (track)?	**En yakın hipodrom nerededir?**	ehn yahkın heepodrom nehrehdehdeer
What's the admission charge?	**Giriş ne kadardır?**	gᵛeereesh neh kahdahrdır
Is there a swimming pool here?	**Burada yüzme havuzu var mı, acaba?**	boorahdah yewzmeh hahvoozoo vahr mı ahjahbah
Is it open-air or indoors?	**Açıkhava mıdır, kapalı mıdır?**	ahchıkhahvah mıdır kahpahlı mıdır
Is it heated?	**Isıtma tertibatı var mıdır?**	ıssıtmah tehrteebahtı vahr mıdır
Can one swim in the lake/river?	**Gölde/Nehirde yüzülür mü?**	gurldeh/nehheerdeh yewzewlewr mew
I'd like to see a (classic) wrestling match.	**Bir yağlı güreş görmek istiyorum.**	beer yahlı gurresh gurmehk eesteeyoroom
Can you get me a couple of tickets?	**Bana iki bilet verebilir misiniz?**	bahnah eekee beeleht vehrehbeeleer meesseeneez
Is there a football (soccer) match anywhere this Saturday?	**Bu cumartesi bir yerde futbol maçı var mı?**	boo joomahrtehssee beer yehrdeh footbol mahchı vahr mı
Who's playing?	**Kimler oynuyor?**	keemlehr oynooyor
Is there any good fishing around here?	**Yakınlarda balık avlıyacak iyi bir yer var mı?**	yahkınlahrdah bahlık ahvlıyahjahk eeyee beer yehr vahr mı
Do I need a permit?	**Avlanma ruhsatına ihtiyaç var mı?**	ahvlahnmah roohhsahtınah eehhteeyahch vahr mı
Where can I get one?	**Nereden alabilirim?**	nehrehdehn ahlahbeeleereem

On the beach

Is it safe for swimming?	Emniyetle yüzülebilir mi?	ehmneeyehtleh yewzewleh beeleer mee
Is there a lifeguard?	Cankurtaran var mıdır?	jahnkoortahrahn vahr mıdır
Is it safe for children?	Çocuklar için emniyetli midir?	chojooklahr eecheen ehmneeyehtlee meedeer
It's very calm.	Çok sakin.	chok sahkeen
There are some big waves.	Bazı büyük dalgalar vardır.	bahzı bewyewk dahlgahlahr vahrdır
Are there any dangerous currents?	Tehlikeli akıntılar var mıdır?	tehhleekehlee ahkıntılahr vahr mıdır
What time is high tide?	Met ne zamandır?	meht neh zahmahndır
What time is low tide?	Cezir ne zamandır?	jehzeer neh zahmahndır
What's the temperature of the water?	Suyun sıcaklığı kaç derecedir?	sooyoon sıjahklı kahch dehrehjehdeer
I want to hire a/an/some...	Bir ... kiralamak istiyorum.	beer ... keerahlahmahk eesteeyoroom
air mattress	deniz yatağı	dehneez yahtahı
bathing hut	kabin	kahbeen
deck-chair	şezlong	shehzlong
skin-diving equipment	sualtı teçhizatı	sooahltı tehchheezahtı
sunshade	güneş şemsiyesi	gᵉwnehsh shehmsee-yehssee
tent	çadır	chahdır
water-skis	su kayağı	soo kayahı
Where can I rent a...?	Nereden bir ... kiralıyabilirim?	nehrehdehn beer ... keerahlıyahbeeleerem
boat	sandal	sahndahl
motor-boat	deniz motoru	dehneez motoroo
rowing-boat	kayık	kahyık
sailing-boat	yelkenli	yehlkehnlee
What's the charge per hour?	Saati kaçadır?	sartı kahchahdir

ÖZEL PLAJ	DENİZE GİRİLMEZ
PRIVATE BEACH	NO BATHING

Winter sports

In winter, you can ski at Ulu Dag near Bursa, at Mount Erciyas, west of Kayseri and at Mount Elma Dag near Ankara. At these and other spots, you can also go mountain climbing.

Is there a skating-rink near here?	**Yakınlarda bir patinaj sahası var mıdır?**	yahkınlahrdah beer pahteenahzh sahhahssı vahr mıdır
I want to hire some skates.	**Paten kiralamak istiyorum.**	pahtehn keerahlahmahk eesteeyoroom
What are the skiing conditions like at Ulu Dag?	**Uludağ'da kayak yapma şartları nasıldır?**	ooloodardah kahyahk yahpmah shahrtlahrı nahssıldır
Can I take skiing lessons there?	**Orada kayak dersleri alabilir miyim?**	orahdah kahyahk dehrslehree ahlahbeeleer meeyeem
Are there ski lifts?	**Telesiyej var mıdır?**	tehlehsseeyehzh vahr mıdır
I want to hire a/some...	**... kiralamak istiyorum.**	... keerahlahmahk eesteeyoroom
ice skates	**Buz pateni**	booz pahtehnee
skiing equipment	**Kayak teçhizatı**	kahyahk tehchheezahtı
sled	**Bir kızak**	beer kızahk
boots	**Çizme**	cheezmeh
poles	**Kayak sopası**	kahyahk sopahssı
skis	**Kayak**	kahyahk

RELAXING

Camping—Countryside

The country's tourism ministry has placed many camping sites into three classes. These are basically rated according to size rather than the facilities offered. Besides these sites, there are many other campgrounds scattered across the country, particularly along the coasts and near tourist centres.

If you want to camp on private land, get permission from the owner first.

English	Turkish	Pronunciation
Can we camp here?	**Burada kamp yapabilir miyiz?**	boorahdah kahmp yahpahbeeleer meeyeez
Where can one camp for the night?	**Gece nerede kamp yapılabilir?**	gᵛehjeh nehrehdeh kahmp yahpılahbeeleer
Is there a camping site near here?	**Yakında mokamp var mı?**	yahkındah mokahmp vahr mı
May we camp in your field?	**Arazinizde kamp yapabilir miyiz?**	ahrahzeeneezdeh kahmp yahpahbeeleer meeyeez
Can we park our caravan (trailer) here?	**Karavanımızı buraya park edebilir miyiz?**	kahrahvahnımızı boorahyah pahrk ehdehbeeleer meeyeez
May we light a fire?	**Ateş yakabilir miyiz?**	ahtehsh yahkahbeeleer meeyeez
Is there drinking water?	**İçme suyu bulunur mu?**	eechmeh sooyoo booloonoor moo
Are there shopping facilities on the site?	**Mokampda alışveriş yerleri var mıdır?**	mokahmpdah ahlıshveh-reesh yehrlehree vahr mıdır
Are there...?	**... var mıdır?**	... vahr mıdır
baths	**Banyo**	bahnyo
showers	**Duş**	doosh
toilets	**Tuvalet**	toovahleht
What's the charge...?	**... kirası ne kadardır?**	... keerahssı neh kahdahrdır
per day	**Günlük**	gᵛewnlewk
per person	**I kişilik**	ı keesheeleek
for a car	**Araba**	ahrahbah
for a tent	**Çadır**	chahdır
for a caravan (trailer)	**Karavan**	kahrahvahn

FOR CAMPING EQUIPMENT, see page 106

| Is there a youth hostel near here? | Çevrede talebe yurdu var mıdır? | chehvrehdeh tahlehbeh yoordoo vahr mıdır |
| Do you know where we might stay for the night? | Geceyi geçirebileceğimiz bir yer biliyor musunuz? | gᵛehjehyee gᵛehcheerehbeelehjeheemeez beer yehr beeleeyor moossoonooz |

| KAMP YAPMAK YASAKTIR | KARAVAN GİREMEZ! |
| NO CAMPING | NO CARAVANS (trailers) |

Landmarks

barn	ahır	ahhır
bridge	köprü	kurprew
brook	dere	dehreh
building	bina	beenah
canal	kanal	kahnahl
church	kilise	keeleesseh
cliff	uçurum	oochooroom
copse	koru	koroo
cottage	küçük ev	kewchewk ehv
crossroads	dörtyol ağzı	durtyol arzı
desert	çöl	churl
farm	çiftlik	cheeftleek
field	tarla	tahrlah
footpath	patika	pahteekah
forest	orman	ormahn
highway	anayol	ahnahyol
hill	tepe	tehpeh
house	ev	ehv
inn	han	hahn
lake	göl	gurl
marsh	bataklık	bahtahklık
moorland	sahra	sahrah
mountain	dağ	dar
mountain range	sıradağ	sırahdar
oasis	vaha	vahhah
path	yaya yolu	yahyah yoloo
peak	zirve	zeerveh
plantation	büyük çiftlik	bewyewk cheeftleek
pond	küçük göl	kewchewk gurl
pool	havuz	hahvooz
railway	demiryolu	dehmeeryoloo
river	nehir	nehheer
road	yol	yol

sea	**deniz**	dehneez
spring	**kaynak**	kahynahk
stream	**dere**	dehreh
swamp	**bataklık**	bahtahklık
track	**patika**	pahteekah
tree	**ağaç**	ahch
valley	**vâdi**	vardee
village	**köy**	kury
vineyard	**bağ**	bah
water	**su**	soo
waterfall	**şelâle**	shelarleh
well	**kuyu**	kooyoo
wood	**koru**	koroo

GİRMEK YASAKTIR

NO TRESPASSING

How far is the next village?	**En yakın köy ne kadar uzaktır?**	ehn yahkın kury neh kahdahr oozahktır
What's the name of this village?	**Bu köyün adı nedir?**	boo kuryewn ahdı nehdeer
Are we on the right road for...?	**... için doğru yolda mıyız?**	... eecheen doroo yoldah mıyız
Where does this road lead to?	**Bu yol nereye gider?**	boo yol nehrehyeh greedehr
Can you show on the map where we are?	**Haritada nerede olduğumuzu gösterebilir misiniz?**	hahreetahdah nehrehdeh oldoomoozoo gurstehrehbeeleer meesseeneez
What's the name of that river?	**Şu nehrin adı nedir?**	shoo nehreen ahdı nehdeer
How high is that mountain?	**Şu dağın yüksekliği ne kadardır?**	shoo dahın yewksehkleeee neh kahdahrdır

And if you're tired of walking, you can always try hitch-hiking—though you may have to wait a long time for a lift.

Can you give me a lift to...?	**Beni ...e kadar götürür müsünüz?**	behnee ...eh kahdahr gurtewrewr mewssewnew...

Making friends

Introduction

Here are a few phrases to get you started:

How do you do?	**Nasılsınız?**	nahssılsınız
Fine, thanks. And you?	**İyiyim, teşekkür ederim. Siz nasılsınız?**	eeyeeyeem tehshehkkewr ehdehreem. seez nahssılsınız
May I introduce Mr. Ahmet?	**Size Ahmet'i tanıştırayım.**	seezeh ahhmehtee tahnıshtırahyım
I'd like you to meet a friend of mine.	**Sizi bir arkadaşımla tanıştırayım.**	seezee beer ahrkahdah-shımlah tahnıshtırahyım
Metin, this is...	**Metin, ... Bey.**	mehteen ... bay
My name's...	**Adım ...'dır.**	ahdım ...dır
Glad to know you.	**Memnun oldum.**	mehmnoon oldoom

Follow-up

How long have you been here?	**Ne zamandan beri buradasınız?**	neh zahmahndahn behree boorahdahssınız
We've been here a week.	**Bir haftadır burdayız.**	beer hahftahdır boordahyız
Is this your first visit?	**Buraya ilk gelişiniz mi?**	boorahyah eelk gʸehleesheeneez mee
No, we came here last year.	**Hayır, geçen sene de gelmiştik.**	hahyır gʸehchehn sehneh deh gʸehlmeeshteek
Are you enjoying your stay?	**Hoşça vakit geçiriyor musunuz?**	hoshchah vahkeet gʸeh-cheereeyor moossoonooz
Yes, I like ... very much.	**... çok hoşuma gidiyor.**	... chok hoshoomah gʸeedeeyor
Where do you come from?	**Nerelisiniz?**	nehrehleesseeneez
What part of... do you come from?	**...'n neresinden-siniz?**	...n nehrehsseendehn-seeneez
I'm from...	**...denim.**	...dehneem

Are you on your own?	**Tek başınıza mısınız?**	tehk bahshınıhzhah mıssınız
I'm with...	**... beraberim.**	... behrahbehreem
my husband	**Eşimle**	ehsheemleh
my wife	**Eşimle**	ehsheemleh
my family	**Ailemle**	aheelehmleh
my parents	**Ebeveynimle**	ehbehvayneemleh
some friends	**Arkadaşlarımla**	ahrkahdahshlahrımlah
Where are you staying?	**Nerede kalıyor-sunuz?**	nehrehdeh kahlıyor-soonooz
I'm a student.	**Öğrenciyim.**	urehnjeeyeem
What are you studying?	**Ne tahsil ediyorsunuz?**	neh tahhseel ehdeeyorsoonooz
We're here on holiday.	**Tatildeyiz.**	tahteeldehyeez
I'm here on a business trip.	**İş seyahatindeyim.**	eesh sehyahhahteendeh-yeem
I hope we'll see you again soon.	**İnşallah tekrar görüşürüz.**	eenshahllahh tehkrahr gurrewshewrewz
See you later/See you tomorrow.	**Tekrar görüşürüz/ Yarın görüşürüz.**	tehkrahr gurrewshewrewz/ yahrın gurrewshewrewz

The weather

They talk about the weather just as much in Turkey as the Americans and British are supposed to do. So...

What a lovely day!	**Ne güzel bir gün!**	neh gᵞewzehl beer gᵞewn
What awful weather!	**Ne kötü bir hava.**	neh kurtew beer hahvah
Isn't it cold today?	**Bugün hava soğuk değil mi?**	boogᵞewn hahvah soook deheel mee
Isn't it hot today?	**Bugün hava sıcak değil mi?**	boogᵞewn hahvah sıjahk deheel mee
Is it usually as warm as this?	**Genellikle böyle sıcak mıdır?**	gᵞehnehlleekleh burleh sıjahk mıdır
Do you think it'll... tomorrow?	**Sizce yarın hava ... olur?**	seezjeh yahrın hahvah ... oloor
rain	**yağmurlu mu**	yahmoorloo moo
snow	**karlı mı**	kahrlı mı
clear up	**açık mı**	ahchık mı
be sunny	**güneşli mi**	gᵞewnehshlee mee

Invitations

My wife and I would like you to dine with us on...	Eşim ve ben sizi, ...akşamı yemeğe davet etmek istiyorduk.	ehsheem veh behn seezee ... ahkshahmı yehmeheh dahveht ehtmehk eesteeyordook
Can you come to dinner tomorrow night?	Yarın akşam yemeğe gelebilir misiniz?	yahrın ahkshahm yehmeheh gʸehlehbeeleer meesseeneez
Can you come over for cocktails this evening?	Bu akşam bir kokteyl içmeye gelebilir misiniz?	boo ahkshahm beer koktayl eechmehyeh gʸehlehbeeleer meesseeneez
There's a party. Are you coming?	Parti var. Siz de geliyor musunuz?	pahrtee vahr. seez deh gʸehleeyor moossoonooz
That's very kind of you.	Çok naziksiniz.	chok narzeekseeneez
Great. I'd love to come.	Fevkalâde. Büyük bir zevkle gelirim.	fehvkahlardeh. bewyewk beer zehvkleh gʸehleereem
What time shall we come?	Saat kaçta gelelim?	sart kahchtah gʸehlehleem
May I bring a friend?	Bir arkadaş getirebilir miyim?	beer ahrkahdahsh gʸehteerehbeeleer meeyeem
I'm afraid we've got to go now.	Maalesef gitmemiz gerekiyor.	mahlehssehf gʸeetmehmeez gʸehrehkeeyor
Next time you must come to visit us.	Gelecek sefere de biz sizi bekleriz.	gʸehlehjehk sehfehreh deh beez seezee behklehreez
Thanks for the evening. It was great.	Bu akşam için çok teşekkürler. Harikulâdeydi.	boo ahkshahm eecheen chok tehshehkkewrlehr. hahreekoolardaydee

Dating

Would you like a cigarette?	Sigara ister misiniz?	seegahrah eestehr meesseeneez
Do you have a light please?	Acaba ateşiniz var mı?	ahjahbah ahtehsheeneez vahr mı
Can I get you a drink?	Size bir içki getirebilirmiyim?	seezeh beer eechkee gʸehteerehbeeleermeeyeem
Are you waiting for someone?	Birisini mi bekliyorsunuz?	beereesseenee mee behkleeyorsoonooz

English	Turkish	Pronunciation
Are you free this evening?	Bu akşam serbest misiniz?	boo ahkshahm sehrbehst meesseeneez
Would you like to go out with me tonight?	Bu akşam benimle çıkar mısınız?	boo ahkshahm behneemleh chıkahr mıssınız
Would you like to go dancing?	Dansa gitmek ister misiniz?	dahnsah gᵛeetmehk eestehr meesseeneez
I know a good discotheque.	İyi bir diskotek biliyorum.	eeyee beer deeskotehk beeleeyoroom
Shall we go to the cinema (movies)?	Sinemaya gidelim mi?	seenehmahyah gᵛeedehleem mee
Would you like to go for a drive?	Arabayla gezmek ister misiniz?	ahrahbahylah gᵛehzmehk eestehr meesseeneez
I'd love to, thank you.	Elbette, teşekkür ederim.	ehlbehtteh tehshehkkewr ehdehreem
Where shall we meet?	Nerede buluşalım?	nehrehdeh boolooshahlım
I'll pick you up at your hotel.	Sizi otelden alırım.	seezee otehldehn ahlırım
I'll phone you at 8.	Saat sekizde telefonla ararım.	sart sehkeezdeh tehlehfonlah ahrahrım
May I take you home?	Sizi evinize götürebilir miyim?	seezee ehveeneezeh gurtewrehbeeleer meeyeem
Can I see you again tomorrow?	Sizi yarın tekrar görebilir miyim?	seezee yahrın tehkrahr gurrehbeeleer meeyeem
Thank you, it's been a wonderful evening.	Çok teşekkür ederim, fevkalâde bir gece geçirdim.	chok tehshehkkewr ehdehreem fehvkahlardeh beer gᵛehjeh gᵛehcheerdeem
I've enjoyed myself tremendously.	Çok hoş vakit geçirdim.	chok hosh vahkeet gᵛehcheerdeem
What's your telephone number?	Telefon numaranız kaç?	tehlehfon noomahrahnız kahch
Do you live with your family?	Ailenizle beraber mi kalıyorsunuz.	aheelehneezleh behrahbehr mee kahlıyorsoonooz
Do you live alone?	Tek başınıza mı oturuyorsunuz?	tehk bahshınızah mı otoorooyorsoonooz
What time is your last train?	En son hangi trene binebilirsiniz?	ehn son hahngᵛee trehneh beenehbeeleerseeneez

Shopping guide

This shopping guide is designed to help you find what you want with ease, accuracy and speed. It features:

1. A list of all major shops, stores and services (p. 98);
2. Some general expressions required when shopping to allow you to be specific and selective (p. 100); and
3. Full details of the shops and services most likely to concern you. Here you'll find advice, alphabetical lists of items and conversion charts listed under the headings below.

		page
Bookshop	books, magazines, newspapers, stationery	104
Camping	camping equipment	106
Chemist's (pharmacy)	medicine, first-aid, cosmetics, toilet articles	108
Clothing	clothes, shoes, accessories	112
Electrical appliances	radios, tape-recorders, razors, records	119
Hairdresser's	barber's, ladies' hairdresser's, beauty salon	121
Jeweller's	jewellery, watches, watch repairs	123
Laundry—Dry cleaning	usual facilities	126
Photography	cameras, accessories, films, developing	127
Provisions	this is confined to basic items required for picnics	129
Souvenirs	souvenirs, gifts, fancy goods	131
Tobacconist's	smoker's supplies	132

SHOPPING GUIDE

Shops, stores and services

Shops are open daily except Sunday from 9 a.m. to 7 p.m. The bustling bazaars will be the most fascinating places on the tourist's shopping spree. There especially you'll have to be ready to haggle for many items, though much merchandise now has a set price. Some bazaars are immense labyrinths where you'll find everything from shoe laces to gold earrings, from potatoes to fine Bursa silk.

Where's the nearest...?	En yakın ... nerededir?	ehn yahkın... nehrehdehdeer
antique shop	antikacı	ahnteekahjı
art gallery	sanat galerisi	sahnaht gahlehreessee
bakery	fırın	fırın
bank	banka	bahnkah
barber's	berber	behrbehr
bazaar	kapalı çarşı	kahpahlı chahrshı
beauty salon	güzellik salonu	gᵛewzehlleek sahlonoo
bookshop	kitabevi	keetahbehvee
bookstall	kitap sergisi	keetahp sehrgᵛeessee
bootblack	ayakkabı boyacısı	ahyahkkahbı boyahjıssı
butcher	kasap	kahssahp
cable office	postahane	postahhahneh
camera store	fotoğrafçı dükkânı	fotorahfchı dewkkarnı
candy store	şekerci dükkânı	shehkehrjee dewkkarnı
chemist's	eczane	ehjzahneh
cigarette stand	sigara bayii	seegahrah bahyee
cobbler	eskici kunduracı	ehskeejee koondoorahjı
confectioner	şekerci	shehkehrjee
dairy	sütçü dükkânı	sewtchew dewkkarnı
delicatessen	şarkütori	sharkewturree
dentist	dişçi	deeshchee
department store	büyük mağaza	bewyewk mahzah
doctor	doktor	doktor
draper	kumaşçı	koomahshchı
dressmaker	terzi	tehrzee
drugstore	eczane	ehjzahneh
dry cleaner	kuru temizleyici	kooroo tehmeezlehyeejee
dry goods store	kumaşçı	koomahshchı
filling station	benzin istasyonu	behnzeen eestahssyonoo
fishmonger's	balıkçı dükkânı	bahlıkchı dewkkarnı
florist	çiçekçi dükkânı	chechehkchee dewkkarnı
furrier	kürkçü dükkânı	kewrkchew dewkkarnı
garage	tamirhane	tahmeerhahneh

greengrocer	manav	mahnahv
grocery	bakkal dükkânı	bahkkahl dewkkarnı
hairdresser's (men)	berber	behrbehr
hairdresser's (ladies)	kuaför	kooahfurr
hardware store	nalbur	nahlboor
hat shop	şapkacı dükkânı	shahpkahjı dewkkarnı
hospital	hastahane	hahsstahhahneh
jeweller's	kuyumcu	kooyoomjoo
launderette	çamaşırcı kadın	chahmahshırjı kahdın
laundry	çamaşırhane	chahmahshırhahneh
leather goods store	derici dükkânı	dehreejee dewkkarnı
liquor store	içki bayii	eechkee bahyee
market	çarşı-pazar	chahrshı-pahzahr
milliner	şapkacı dükkanı	shahpkahjı dewkkarnı
newsagent	gazeteci	gahzehtehjee
news-stand	gazete bayii	gahzehteh bahyee
off-licence	içki bayii	eechkee bahyee
optician	göz doktoru	gurz doktoroo
pastry shop	tatlıcı dükkânı	tahtljı dewkkarnı
petrol station	benzin istasyonu	behnzeen eestahssyonoo
photographer	fotoğrafçı	fotorahfchı
photo shop	fotoğrafçı dükkânı	fotorahfchı dewkkarnı
police station	karakol	kahrahkol
post office	postahane	postahhahneh
shirt-maker's	gömlekçi	gurmlehkchee
shoemaker's (repairs)	kunduracı	koondoorahjı
shoe shop	ayakkabı mağazası	ahyahkkahbı mahzahssı
souvenir shop	hâtıra eşyası satan dükkân	hartırah ehshyahssı sahtahn dewkkarn
sporting goods shop	spor mağazası	spor mahzahssı
stationer's	kırtasiyeci	kırtahsseeyehjee
supermarket	süpermarket	sewpehrmahrkeht
sweet shop	şekerci dükkânı	shehkehrjee dewkkarnı
tailor	terzi	tehrzee
tea room	çayevi	chahyehvee
telegraph office	postahane	postahhahneh
tobacconist's	tütün satıcısı	tewtewn sahtıjıssı
toy shop	oyuncakçı dükkânı	oyoonjahkchı dewkkarnı
travel agent	seyahat acentası	sehyahhaht ahjehntahssı
vegetable store	manav	mahnahv
veterinarian	veteriner	vehtehreenehr
watch maker's	saatçı	sartchı
wine merchant	şarap tüccarı	shahrahp tewjjahrı

İNDİRİMLİ SATIŞ	SALE

General expressions

Here are some expressions which will be useful to you when you're out shopping:

Where?

Where can I find a...?	Nerede bir ... bulabilirim?	nehrehdeh beer ... boolahbeeleereem
Where do they sell...?	... nerede satılır?	... nehrehdeh sahtılır
Can you recommend an inexpensive...?	Ucuz bir...tavsiye edebilir misiniz?	oojooz beer...tahvseeyeh ehdehbeeleer meesseenee
Where's the main shopping area?	Alış veriş merkezi nerededir?	ahlısh vehreesh mehrkehzee nehrehdehdee
How far is it from here?	Buradan ne kadar uzaktadır?	boorahdahn neh kahdahr oozahktahdır
How do I get there?	Oraya nasıl gidebilirim?	orahyah nahssıl gⁱeedehbeeleereem

Service

Can you help me?	Bana yardım edebilir misiniz?	bahnah yahrdım ehdehbeeleer meesseenee
I'm just looking around.	Şöyle bir bakıyorum.	shurleh beer bahkıyoroom
I want...	... istiyorum.	... eesteeyoroom
Can you show me some...?	Bana birkaç ... gösterebilir misiniz?	bahnah beerkahch ... gurstehrehbeeleer meesseeneez
Do you have any...?	... var mı?	... vahr mı

That one

Can you show me...?	... gösterebilir misiniz?	... gurstehrehbeeleer meesseeneez
that/those	Onu/Onları	onoo/onlahrı
the one in the window	Vitrindekini	veetreendhekeenee
the one in the display case	Camekânın içindekini	jahmehkarnın eecheendhe keenee
It's over there.	Orada.	orahdah

Defining the article

I want a … one.	… bir tane istiyorum.	… beer tahneh eesteeyoroom
big	Büyük	bewyewk
cheap	Ucuz	oojooz
dark	Koyu	koyoo
good	İyi	eeyee
heavy	Ağır	ahır
large	Büyük	bewyewk
light (weight)	Hafif	hahfeef
light (colour)	Açık renk	ahchık rehnk
oval	Oval	ovahl
rectangular	Dikdörtgen	deekdurtgᵛehn
round	Yuvarlak	yoovahrlahk
small	Küçük	kewchewk
square	Kare	kahreh
I don't want anything too expensive.	Fazla pahalı bir şey istemiyorum.	fahzlah pahhahlı beer shay eestehmeeyoroom

Preference

I prefer something of better quality.	Daha kaliteli bir şey tercih ederim.	dahhah kahleetehlee beer shay tehrjeehh ehdehreem
Can you show me some more?	Daha başkalarını gösterebilir misiniz?	dahhah bahshkahlahrını gurstehrehbeeleer meesseeneez
Haven't you anything…?	… birşey yok mu?	… beershay yok moo
cheaper/better	Daha ucuz/Daha pahalı	dahhah oojooz/dahhah pahhahlı
larger/smaller	Daha büyük/Daha küçük	dahhah bewyewk/dahhah kewchewk

How much?

How much is this?	Bu kaçadır?	boo kahchahdır
I don't understand.	Anlamıyorum.	anlahmıyoroom
Please write it down.	Lütfen yazar mısınız?	lewtfehn yahzahr mıssınız
I don't want to spend more than … liras.	… liradan fazla harcamak istemiyorum.	… leerahdahn fahzlah harjahmahk eestehmeeyoroom

FOR COLOURS, see page 113

Decision

That's just what I want.	**Bu tam benim istediğim.**	boo tahm behneem eestehdeeeem
It's not quite what I want.	**Tam olarak istediğim değil.**	tahm olahrahk eestehdeeeem deheel
No, I don't like it.	**Hayır, bunu beğenmedim.**	hahyir boonoo behehnmehdeem
I'll take it.	**Bunu alacağım.**	boonoo ahlahjahım

Ordering

| Can you order it for me? | **Bunu bana sipariş eder misiniz?** | boonoo bahnah seepah- reesh ehdehr meesseeneez |
| How long will it take? | **Ne kadar sürer?** | neh kahdahr sewrehr |

Delivery

I'll take it with me.	**Kendim götürürüm.**	kehndeem gurtewrewrewm
Deliver it to the... Hotel.	**... Oteli'ne teslim edin.**	... otehleeneh tehsleem ehdeen
Please send it to this address.	**Lütfen şu adrese gönderin.**	lewtfehn shoo ahdrehsseh gurndehreen
Will I have any difficulty with the customs?	**Gümrükte herhangi bir zorlukla karşıla- şabilir miyim?**	gewmrewkteh hehrhahng bir zorlooklah kahrshilah- shahbeeleer meeyeem

Paying

How much is it?	**Ne kadardır?**	neh kahdahrdır
Can I pay by traveller's cheque?	**Seyahat çekiyle ödeyebilir miyim?**	sehyahhaht chehkeeyleh urdehyehbeeleer meeyeem
Do you accept dollars/ pounds/credit cards?	**Dolar/Sterlin/kredi kartı kabul eder misiniz?**	dolahr/stehrleen/krehdee kahrtı kahbool ehdehr meesseeneez
Haven't you made a mistake in the bill?	**Hesapta bir yanlışlık yok mu?**	hehssahptah beer yahnlıshlık yok moo
Can I please have a receipt?	**Bir fatura yazar mısınız?**	beer fahtoorah yahzahr mıssınız
Will you please wrap it?	**Sarıverin, lütfen.**	sahrıvehreen lewtfehn

Anything else?

No, thanks, that's all.	Hayır, hepsi bu kadar, teşekkür ederim.	hahyır hehpsee boo kahdahr tehshehkkewr ehdehreem
Yes, I want...	Evet, ... istiyorum.	ehveht ... eesteeyoroom
Thank you. Goodbye.	Teşekkür ederim. Allahaısmarladık.	tehshehkkewr ehdehreem. ahllahhahısmahrlahdık

Dissatisfied

Can you please exchange this?	Şunu değiştirebilir misiniz, lütfen?	shoonoo deheeshteerehbeeleer meesseeneez lewtfehn
I want to return this.	Şunu geri vermek istiyorum.	shoonoo gᵛehree vehrmehk eesteeyoroom
I'd like a refund. Here's the receipt.	Paramı iade eder misiniz? İşte fatura.	pahrahmı eeahdeh ehdehr meesseeneez eeshteh fahtoorah

SHOPPING GUIDE

Size yardım edebilir miyim?	Can I help you?
Ne arzu edersiniz?	What would you like?
Ne renk istersiniz?	What colour would you like?
Hangi şekli istersiniz?	What shape would you like?
Hangi kalite arzu edersiniz?	What quality would you like?
Ne kadar istersiniz?	How much (many) would you like?
Maalesef bulunmaz.	I'm sorry, we haven't any.
Maalesef kalmadı.	We're out of stock.
Onu sizin için sipariş edelim mi?	Shall we order it for you?
Kendiniz mi alırsınız, yoksa evinize mi gönderelim?	Will you take it with you or shall we send it?
Başka birşey var mı?	Anything else?
... lira lütfen.	That's ... liras, please.
Kasa orada.	The cashier's over there.

Bookshop—Stationer's—News-stand

In Turkey bookshops and stationers' are usually separate shops. Newspapers and magazines are sold at news-stands.

Where's the nearest...?	En yakın ... nerededir?	ehn yahkın ... nehrehdehdeer
bookshop	kitabevi	keetahbehvee
stationer's	kırtasiye mağazası	kırtahsseeyeh mahzahssı
news-stand	gazete bayii	gahzehteh bahyee
Can you recommend a good bookshop?	İyi bir kitabevi tavsiye edebilir misiniz?	eeyee beer keetahbehvee tahvseeyeh ehdehbeeleer meesseeneez
Where can I buy an English newspaper?	Nereden bir ingiliz gazetesi alabilirim?	nehrehdehn beer eengveeleez gahzehtehssee ahlahbeeleereem
I want to buy a / an / some ...	...almak istiyorum.	... ahlmahk eesteeyoroom
address book	Bir adres defteri	beer ahdrehss dehftehree
ball-point pen	Bir tükenmez kalem	beer tewkehnmehz kahlehm
book	Bir kitap	beer keetahp
box of paints	Bir suluboya takımı	beer soolooboyah tahkımı
carbon paper	Karbon kâğıdı	kahrbon kardı
cellophane tape	Seloteyp	sehlotayp
crayons	Birkaç kurşun kalem	beerkahch koorshoon kahlehm
dictionary	Bir sözlük	beer surzlewk
Turkish-English	Türkçe-İngilizce	tewrkcheh eengveeleezjeh
English-Turkish	İngilizce-Türkçe	eengveeleezjeh tewrkcheh
pocket dictionary	Cep sözlüğü	jehp surzlew
drawing paper	Resim kâğıdı	rehsseem kardı
drawing pins	Raptiye	rahpteeyeh
envelopes	Birkaç zarf	beerkahch zahrf
eraser	Bir silgi	beer seelgvee
exercice book	Bir defter	beer dehftehr
fountain pen	Bir dolmakalem	beer dolmahkahlehm
glue	Tutkal	tootkahl
grammar book	Bir gramer kitabı	beer grahmehr keetahbı
guide-book	Bir rehber kitabı	beer rehhbehr keetahbı
ink	Mürekkep	mewrehkkehp
black/red/blue	siyah/kırmızı/mavi	seeyahh/kırmızı/mahvee
labels	Birkaç etiket	beerkahch ehteekeht
magazine	Bir mecmua	beer mehjmooah

map	**Bir harita**	beer hahreetah
map of the town	**şehir planı**	shehheer plahnı
road map of...	**...'nın karayolları haritası**	...nın kahrahyollahrı hahreetahssı
newspaper	**Bir ... gazetesi**	beer ... gahzehtehssee
American/English	**Amerikan/İngiliz**	ahmehreekahn/ eengᵛeeleez
notebook	**Bir defter**	beer dehftehr
note paper	**Mektup kâğıdı**	mehktoop kardı
paperback	**Cep kitabı**	jehp keetahbı
paper napkins	**Kâğıt peçete**	kart pehchehteh
paste	**Kola**	kolah
pen	**Kalem**	kahlehm
pencil	**Bir kurşun kalem**	beer koorshoon kahlem
pencil sharpener	**Bir kalemtraş**	beer kahlehmtrahsh
playing cards	**Oyun kâğıdı**	oyoon kardı
postcards	**Birkaç kartpostal**	beerkahch kahrtpostahl
refill (for a pen)	**Yedek kalemiçi**	yehdehk kahlehmeechee
rubber	**Bir silgi**	beer seelgᵛee
ruler	**Bir cetvel**	beer jehtvehl
sketching block	**Bir resim defteri**	beer rehsseem dehftehree
string	**Sicim**	seejeem
thumbtacks	**Raptiye**	rahpteeyeh
tissue paper	**İpek kâğıt**	eepehk kart
tracing paper	**Kopya kâğıdı**	kopyah kardı
typewriter ribbon	**Bir daktilo şeridi**	beer dahkteelo shehreedee
typing paper	**Daktilo kâğıdı**	dahkteelo kardı
writing pad	**Bir blok-not**	beer bloknot
Where's the guidebook section?	**Rehber kitapları reyonu nerededir?**	rehhbehr keetahplahrı rehyonoo nehrehdehdeer
Where do you keep the English books?	**İngilizce kitaplar nerede bulunuyor?**	eengᵛeeleezjeh keetahplahr nehrehdeh booloonooyor
Have you any of...'s books in English?	**...'ın ingilizce basılmış kitapları var mı?**	...ın eengᵛeeleezjeh bahssılmısh keetahplahrı vahr mı
Is there an English translation of...?	**...'ın ingilizce baskısı var mı?**	...ın eengᵛeeleezjeh bahskıssı vahr mı

Here are some contemporary Turkish authors whose books are available in English translation:

Halide Edip Adıvar	**Nâzım Hikmet**
Ekrem Akurgal	**Aziz Nesin**
Yahya Kemal	**Yaşar Kemal**
Beyatlı	

Camping

Here we're concerned with the equipment you may need.

I'd like a/an/some...	... istiyorum.	... eesteeyoroom
axe	Balta	bahltah
bottle-opener	Şişe açacağı	sheesheh ahchahjahı
bucket	Kova	kovah
butane gas	Butan gazı	bootahn gahzı
camp-bed	Kamp yatağı	kahmp yahtarı
camping equipment	Kamping malzemesi	kahmpeeng mahlzeh-mehssee
can opener	Konserve açacağı	konsehrveh ahchahjahı
candles	Mum	moom
chair	Sandalye	sahndahlyeh
folding chair	Açılır kapanır iskemle	ahchılır kahpahnır eeskehmleh
compass	Pusula	poossoolah
corkscrew	Tirbuşon	teerbooshon
crockery	Çanak-çömlek	chahnahk-churmlehk
cutlery	Çatal-bıçak	chahtahl-bıchahk
deck-chair	Şezlong	shehzlong
first-aid kit	İlk yardım çantası	eelk yahrdım chahntahssı
fishing tackle	Balık avı takımı	bahlık ahvı tahkımı
flashlight	El feneri	ehl fehnehree
frying-pan	Tava	tahvah
groundsheet	Plastik çadır halısı	plahsteek chahdır hahlıssı
hammer	Çekiç	chehkeech
hammock	Hamak	hahmahk
haversack	Kamping çantası	kahmpeeng chahntahssı
ice-bag	Buz torbası	booz torbahssı
kerosene	Gaz yağı	gahz yahı
kettle	Güğüm	gewewm
knapsack	Sırt çantası	sırt chahntahssı
lamp	Lâmba	larmbah
lantern	Fener	fehnehr
matches	Kibrit	keebreet
mattress	Şilte	sheelteh
methylated spirits	İspirto	eespeerto
mosquito net	Cibinlik	jeebeenleek
pail	Kova	kovah
paraffin	Gaz yağı	gahz yahı
penknife	Çakı	chahkı
picnic case	Piknik çantası	peekneek chahntahssı
pressure cooker	Düdüklü tencere	dewdewklew tehnjehreh
primus stove	Kamping ocağı	kahmpeeng ojahı

rope	İp	eep
rucksack	Sırt çantası	sırt chahntahssı
saucepan	Saplı tencere	sahplı tehnjehreh
scissors	Makas	mahkahss
screwdriver	Tornavida	tornahveedah
sheathknife	Kınlı büyük bıçak	kınlı bewyewk bıchahk
sleeping bag	Uyku tulumu	ooykoo tooloomoo
stewpan	Yahni tenceresi	yahhnee tehnjehrehssee
stove	Soba	sobah
table	Masa	mahssah
folding table	Portatif masa	portahteef mahssah
tent	Çadır	chahdır
tent-peg	Çadır kazığı	chahdır kahzıı
tent-pole	Çadır direği	chahdır deerehee
thermos flask (bottle)	Termos	tehrmoss
tin-opener	Konserve açacağı	konsehrveh ahchahjahı
tongs	Maşa	mahshah
tool kit	Âlet çantası	arleht chahntahssı
torch	El feneri	ehl fehnehree
water carrier	Su tulumu	soo tooloomoo
wood alcohol	İspirto	eespeerto

Dishes

beaker (tumbler)	tas	tahss
cup	fincan	feenjahn
food box	yiyecek kutusu	yeeyehjehk kootoossoo
mug	bardak	bahrdahk
plate	tabak	tahbahk
saucer	fincan tabağı	feenjahn tahbahı

Cutlery

fork	çatal	chahtahl
knife	bıçak	bıchahk
dessert knife	pasta bıçağı	pahstah bıchahı
spoon	kaşık	kahshık
teaspoon	çay kaşığı	chahy kahshıı
(made of) plastic	plastikten (yapılmış)	plahsteektehn (yahpılmısh)
(made of) stainless steel	paslanmaz çelikten (yapılmış)	pahslahnmahz chehleektehn (yahpılmısh)

Chemist's—Drugstore

The chemist's in Turkey normally doesn't stock the great range of medicine and merchandise that we find back home. For perfume and cosmetics, you must go to a *parfümeri*.

In the window you'll see a notice telling you where the nearest all-night chemist's is.

This section has been divided into two parts:

1. Pharmaceutical—medicine, first-aid, etc.
2. Toiletry—toilet articles, cosmetics

General

Where's the nearest (all-night) chemist's?	**En yakın (nöbetçi) eczane nerededir?**	ehn yahkın (nurbehtchee) ehjzahneh nehrehdehdeer
What time does the chemist's open/close?	**Eczane ne zaman açılır/ne zaman kapanır?**	ehjzahneh neh zahmahn ahchılır/neh zahmahn kahpahnır

Part 1—Pharmaceutical

I want something for...	**... için birşey istiyorum.**	... eecheen beershay eesteeyoroom
a cold/a cough	**Nezle/Öksürük**	nehzleh/urksewrewk
hay fever	**Saman nezlesi**	sahmahn nehzlehssee
a hangover	**İçki mahmurluğu**	eechkee mahhmoorlooo
sunburn	**Güneş yanığı**	gʼewnehsh yahnıı
travel sickness	**Yol tutması**	yol tootmahssı
an upset stomach	**Mide bozulması**	meedeh bozoolmahssı
Can you make up this prescription for me?	**Bana bu reçeteyi hazırlar mısınız?**	bahnah boo rehchehtehyee hahzırlahr mıssınız
Shall I wait?	**Bekleyebilir miyim?**	behklehyehbeeleer-meeyeem
When shall I come back?	**Tekrar ne zaman uğrayayım?**	tehkrahr neh zahmahn oorahyahyım
Can I get it without a prescription?	**Reçetesiz alabilir miyim?**	rehchehtehsseez ahlahbeeleer meeyeem

FOR DOCTOR, see page 162

Can I have a/an some...?	... istiyorum.	... eesteeyoroom
ammonia	**Nişadır**	neeshadır
antiseptic cream	**Antiseptik krem**	ahnteessehpteek krehm
aspirin	**Aspirin**	ahspeereen
bandage	**Sargı bezi**	sahrgı behzee
Band-Aids	**Salvelox**	sahlveh**lokss**
calcium tablets	**Kalsiyum tabletleri**	kahl**see**yoom tahb**leht**lehree
chlorine tablets	**Klorin tabletleri**	kloreen tahb**leht**lehree
contraceptives	**Doğum kontrol hapı**	dooom kontrol hahpı
corn plasters	**Nasır yakısı**	nahssır yahkıssı
cotton wool	**İdrofil pamuk**	eedrofeel pahmook
cough drops	**Öksürük damlası**	urksewrwek dahmlahssı
diabetic lozenges	**Sakarin**	sahkahreen
disinfectant	**Dezenfektan**	dehzehnfehktahn
ear drops	**Kulak damlası**	koolahk dahmlahssı
Elastoplast	**Salvelox**	sahlveh**lokss**
first-aid kit	**İlkyardım çantası**	eelkyahrdım chahntahssı
flea powder	**Pirelere karşı pudra**	peerehlehreh kahrshı poodrah
gargle	**Gargara**	gahrgahrah
gauze	**Gazlı bez**	gahzlı behz
insect lotion	**Böcek sokmalarına karşı merhem**	burjehk sokmahlahrınah kahrshı mehrhehm
insect repellent	**Böceklerden korunmak için krem**	burjehklehrdehn
iodine	**Tentürdiod**	tehntewrdeeod
iron pills	**Demir hapı**	dehmeer hahpı
laxative	**Müshil**	mewsheel
lint	**Gazlı bez**	gahzlı behz
mouthwash	**Gargara**	gahrgahrah
quinine tablets	**Kinin hapı**	keeneen hahpı
sanitary napkins	**Tampon**	tahmpon
sleeping pills	**Uyku hapı**	ooykoo hahpı
stomach pills	**Mide hapı**	meedeh hahpı
thermometer	**Derece**	dehrehjeh
throat lozenges	**Boğaz hapı**	boahz hahpı
tissues	**Kağıt mendil**	kart mehndeel
tranquillizers	**Müsekkin**	mewssehkkeen
vitamin pills	**Vitamin hapı**	veetahmeen hahpı

ZEHİR! POISON!
HÂRİCEN KULLANILIR FOR EXTERNAL USE ONLY

Part 2—Toiletry

I'd like a/an/some...	... istiyorum.	... eesteeyoroom
acne-cream	Ergenliğe karşı krem	ehrgvehnleeeh kahrshı krehm
after-shave lotion	Traş losyonu	trahsh lossyonoo
bath essence	Banyo esansı	bahnyo ehssahnsı
bath salts	Banyo tuzu	bahnyo toozoo
cologne	Kolonya	kolonyah
cream	Krem	krehm
cleansing cream	Makyaj temizleme sütü	mahkyakzk tehmeez-lehmeh sewtew
cold cream	Güzellik kremi	gvewzehlleek krehmee
cuticle cream	Tırnak kremi	tırnahk krehmee
foundation cream	Fondöten	fondurtehn
moisturizing cream	Nemlendirici krem	nehmlehndeereejee krehm
night cream	Gece kremi	gvehjeh krehmee
cuticle remover	Tırnak derisini almak için krem	tırnahk dehreesseenee ahlmahk eecheen krehm
deodorant	Deodoran	dehodorahn
emery board	Tırnak törpüsü	tırnahk turrpewssew
eye liner	Eyeliner	ahylighnehr
eye pencil	Göz kalemi	gurz kahlehmee
eye shadow	Far	fahr
face flannel	Makyaj havlusu	mahkyahzh hahvloossoo
face pack	Yüz maskesi	yewz mahskehssee
face powder	Taş pudra	tahsh poodrah
foot cream/deodorant	Ayak kremi / deodoranı	ahyahk krehmee / dehodorahnı
hand cream/lotion	El kremi/losyonu	ehl krehmee/lossyonoo
Kleenex	Kâğıt mendil	kart mehndeel
lipsalve	Krem şeklinde dudak boyası	krehm shehkleendeh doodahk boyaksı
lipstick	Ruj	roozh
lipstick brush	Dudak fırçası	doodahk fırchahssı
make-up remover	Makyaj silme	mahkyahzh seelmeh
pads	pamuğu	pahmoo
mascara	Rimel	reemehl
nail brush	Tırnak fırçası	tırnahk fırchahssı
nail clippers	Tırnak makası	tırnahk mahkahssı
nail file	Madeni tırnak törpüsü	mahdehnee tırnahk turrpewssew
nail polish	Tırnak cilâsı	tırnahk jeelarssı
nail polish remover	Aseton	ahssehton
nail scissors	Tırnak makası	tırnahk mahkahssı

oil	Yağ	yah
perfume	Koku	kokoo
powder	Pudra	poodrah
powder puff	Pudra ponponu	poodrah ponponoo
rouge	Far	fahr
safety pins	Çengelli iğne	chengᵛehllee eeneh
shampoo	Şampuan	shahmpooah
shaving brush	Traş fırçası	trahsh fırchahssı
shaving cream	Traş kremi	trahsh krehmee
shaving soap	Traş sabunu	trahsh sahboonoo
soap	Sabun	sahboon
sponge	Sünger	sewngᵛehr
sun-tan cream/oil	Güneş kremi/yağı	gᵛewnehsh krehmee/yahı
talcum powder	Talk pudrası	tahlk poodrahssı
tissues	Kâğıt mendil	kart mehndeel
toilet paper	Tuvalet kâğıdı	toovahleht kardı
toilet water	Odötuvalet	odurtoovahleht
toothbrush	Diş fırçası	deesh fırchahssı
toothpowder	Diş macunu	deesh mahjoonoo
towel	Havlu	hahvloo
tweezers	Cımbız	jimbız
washcloth	Makyaj havlusu	mahkyahzh hahvloossoo

For your hair

brush	Fırça	fırchah
comb	Tarak	tahrahk
dye/tint	Saç boyası	sahch boyahssı
grips (bobby pins)	Pens	pehnss
lacquer/spray	Saç spreyi	sahch sprayı
net	Saç filesi	sahch feelehssee
pins	Firkete	feerkehteh
rollers (curlers)	Bigudi	beegoodee
setting lotion	Saç losyonu	sahch lossyonoo
wig	Peruka	pehrookah

For the baby

beaker (tumbler)	Tas	tahss
bib	Önlük	urnlewk
dummy (pacifier)	Emzik	ehmzeek
food	Mama	mahmah
nappies (diapers)	Çocuk bezi	chojook behzee
nappy pins	Çengelli iğne	chengᵛehllee eeneh
plastic pants	Plastik çocuk donu	plahsteek chojook donoo
powder	Talk pudrası	tahlk poodrahssı

Clothing

If you want to buy something specific, prepare yourself in advance. Look at the list of clothing on page 117. Get some idea of the colour, material and size you want. They're all listed on the next few pages.

General

I'd like...	... istiyorum.	... eesteeyoroom
I want...for a 10 year-old boy.	**10 yaşında bir çocuk için ... istiyorum.**	10 yahshındah beer chojook eecheen ... eesteeyoroom
I want something like this.	**Bunun gibi bir şey istiyorum.**	boonoon gᵛeebee beer shay eesteeyoroom
I like the one in the window.	**Vitrindekini istiyorum.**	veetreendehkeenee eesteeyoroom
How much is that per metre?	**Metresi kaça?**	mehtrehssee kahchah

1 centimetre = 0.39 in.	1 inch = 2.54 cm.
1 metre = 39.37 in.	1 foot = 30.5 cm.
10 metres = 32.81 ft.	1 yard = 0.91 m.

Colour

I want something in...	**... birşey istiyorum.**	... beershay eesteeyoroom
I want a darker shade.	**Bir ton koyusunu istiyorum.**	beer ton koyoossoonoo eesteeyoroom
I want something to match this.	**Buna asorti birşey istiyorum.**	boonah ahssortee birshay eesteeyoroom
I don't like the colour.	**Rengini beğenmedin.**	rehngᵛeenee behehnmehdeem

fantezi
(fahntehzee)

kareli
(kahrehlee)

noktalı
(noktahlı)

çizgili
(cheezgᵛeelee)

beige	bej	behzh
black	siyah	seeyahh
blue	mavi	mahvee
brown	kahverengi	kahhvehrehng^yee
cream	krem rengi	krehm rehng^yee
crimson	koyu kırmızı	koyoo kırmızı
emerald	zümrüt yeşili	zewmrewt yehsheelee
fawn	çok açık kahverengi	chok ahchık kahhvehrehng^yee
gold	altın sarısı	ahltın sarıssı
green	yeşil	yehsheel
grey	gri	gree
mauve	mor	mor
orange	turuncu	tooroonjoo
pink	pembe	pehmbeh
purple	erguvan rengi	ehrgoovahn rehng^yee
red	kırmızı	kırmızı
scarlet	al	ahl
silver	gümüş rengi	g^yewmewsh rehng^yee
tan	kestane	kehstahneh
turquoise	türkuvaz	tewrkoovahz
white	beyaz	behyahz
yellow	sarı	sahrı

SHOPPING GUIDE

Material

I want a cotton blouse.	Pamuklu şömiziye istiyorum.	pahmookloo shurmeezeeyeh eesteeyoroom
Do you have anything in…?	… birşeyiniz var mı?	… beershayeeneez vahr mı
I want a cotton blouse.	Pamuklu şömiziye istiyorum.	pahmookloo shurmeezeeyeh eesteeyoroom
Is that hand-made?	El yapısı mıdır?	ehl yahpıssı mıdır
Is that imported?	İthâl malı mıdır?	eethahl mahlı mıdır
Is that made here?	Yerli malı mıdır?	yehrlee mahlı mıdır
I want something thinner.	Daha ince birşey istiyorum.	dahhah eenjeh beershay eesteeyoroom
Do you have any better quality?	Daha kaliteli birşeyiniz var mı?	dahhah kahleetehlee beershayeeneez vahr mı
What's it made of?	Bu neden yapılmıştır?	boo nehdehn yahpılmıshtır

It may be made of...

camel hair	deve tüyü	dehveh tewyew
chiffon	şifon	sheefon
corduroy	fitilli kadife	feeteellee kahdeefeh
cotton	pamuklu	pahmookloo
crepe	krep	krehp
denim	blucin kumaşı	bloojeen koomahshı
felt	keçe	kehcheh
flannel	flanel	flahnehl
gabardine	gabardin	gahbahrdeen
lace	dantel	dahntehl
leather	deri	dehree
linen	keten	kehtehn
needlecord	örgü yünü	urrgʸew yewnew
pique	pike	peekeh
poplin	poplin	popleen
rayon	suni ipekli	soonee eepehklee
satin	saten	sahtehn
sheepskin	koyun postu	koyoon postoo
silk	ipek	eepehk
suede	süed	sewehd
taffeta	tafta	tahftah
terrycloth	havlı kumaş	hahvlı koomahsh
towelling	havluluk kumaş	hahvloolook koomahsh
tulle	tül	tewl
tweed	tüvid	tewveed
velvet	kadife	kahdeefeh
velveteen	taklit kadife	tahkleet kahdeefeh
wool	yün	yewn
worsted	yün ipliği	yewn eepleeee

Size

My size is 38.	38 beden giyiyorum.	38 behdehn gʸeeyeeyoroom
Could you measure me?	Ölçülerimi alır mısınız?	urlchewlehreemee ahlır mıssınız
I don't know the Turkish sizes.	Türkiye'deki bedenleri bilmiyorum.	tewrkeeyehdehkee behdehnlehree beelmeeyoroom

In that case, look at the charts on the next page.

This is your size

Ladies

Dresses/suits						
American	10	12	14	16	18	20
British	32	34	36	38	40	42
Turkish	30	32	34	36	38	40

Stockings							Shoes					
American }	8	8½	9	9½	10	10½	5½	6½	7½	8½	9½	
British }							4	5	6	7	8	
Turkish	0	1	2	3	4	5	37	38	39	40	41	

Gentlemen

Suits/overcoats							Shirts			
American }	36	38	40	42	44	46	15	16	17	18
British }										
Turkish	46	48	50	52	54	56	38	41	43	45

Shoes								
American }	6	7	8	8½	9	9½	10	11
British }								
Turkish	38	40	41	42	43	43	44	45

A good fit?

Can I try it on?	Bunları deneyebilir miyim?	boonlahrı dehnehyeh-beeleer meeyeem
Where's the fitting room?	Kabin nerededir?	kahbeen nehrehdehdeer
Is there a mirror?	Ayna var mı?	ahynah vahr mı
Does it fit?	Üstüme uydu mu?	ewstewmeh ooydoo moo
It fits very well.	Çok iyi uydu.	chok eeyee ooydoo
It doesn't fit.	Uymuyor.	ooymooyor

FOR NUMBERS, see page 175

SHOPPING GUIDE

It's too...	Çok...	chok
short/long	kısa/uzun	kıssah/oozoon
tight/loose	dar/geniş	dahr/g^yehneesh
How long will it take to alter?	Değiştirmesi ne kadar zaman sürer?	deheeshteermehssee neh kahdahr zahmahn sewreh

Shoes

I'd like a pair of...	Bir çift ... istiyorum.	beer cheeft ... eesteeyoroom
shoes/sandals	ayakkabı/sandal	ahyahkkahbı/sahndahl
boots/slippers	bot/terlik	bot/tehrleek
These are too...	Çok...	chok
narrow/wide	dar/geniş	dahr/g^yehneesh
large/small	büyük/küçük	bewyewk/kewchewk
They pinch my toes.	Parmaklarımın ucunu sıkıyor.	pahrmahklahrımın oojoonoo sıkıyor
Do you have a larger size?	Daha büyük numarası yok mu?	dahhah bewyewk noomahrahssı yok moo
I want a smaller size.	Daha küçük numarasını istiyorum.	dahhah kewchewk noomahrahssını eesteeyoroon
Do you have the same in...?	Aynısının ... var mı?	ahynıssının... vahr mı
brown/beige	kahverengisi/beji	kahvehrehng^yeessee/behzhee
black/white	siyahı/beyazı	seeyahhı/behyahzı
I'd like a shine.	Ayakkabı cilâsı istiyorum.	ahyahkkahbı jeelarssı eesteeyoroom

Shoes worn out? Here's the key to getting them fixed again

Can you repair these shoes?	Bu ayakkabıları tamir edebilir misiniz?	boo ahyahkkahbılahrı tahmeer ehdehbeeleer meesseeneez
Can you stitch this?	Bunu dikebilir misiniz?	boonoo deekehbeeleer meesseeneez
I want new soles and heels.	Tam pençe istiyorum.	tahm pehncheh eesteeyoroom
When will they be ready?	Ne zamana hazır olur?	neh zahmahnah hahzır oloor

Clothes and accessories

I would like a/an some...	... istiyorum.	... eesteeyoroom
bathing cap	Bone	boneh
bathing suit	Mayo	mahyo
bath robe	Bornoz	bornoz
bikini	Bikini	beekeenee
blouse	Şömiziye	shurmeezeeyeh
bra	Sutyen	sootyehn
braces (Br.)	Pantolon askısı	pahntahlon ahskıssı
briefs	Külot	kewlot
cap	Kasket	kahskeht
cape	Pelerin	pehlehreen
cardigan	Yelek	yehlehk
coat	Palto	pahlto
dinner jacket	Smokin	smokeen
dress	Rop	rop
dressing gown	Ropdöşambr	ropdurshahmbr
evening dress	Gece elbisesi	gʸehjeh ehlbeessehssee
fur coat	Kürk manto	kewrk mahnto
girdle	Kuşak	kooshahk
gloves	Eldiven	ehldeevehn
gym shoes	Jimnastik ayakkabısı	zheemnahsteek ahyahkkahbıssı
handkerchief	Mendil	mehndeel
hat	Şapka	shahpkah
jacket	Ceket	jehkeht
jeans	Blucin	bloojeen
jumper (Br.)	Kazak	kahzahk
jumper (Am.)	Kolsuz rop	kolsooz rop
lingerie	Kadın çamaşırı	kahdın chahmahshırı
nightdress	Gecelik	gʸehjehleek
overalls	Tulum	tooloom
overcoat	Pardösü	pardurssew
panties	Külot	kewlot
panty-girdle	Külot-korse	kewlot-korseh
panty hose	Külot-çorap	kewlot-chorahp
petticoat	Kombinezon	kombeenehzon
pinafore	Kolsuz rop	kolsooz rop
pyjamas	Pijama	peezhahmah
raincoat	Yağmurluk	yahmoorlook
rubber boots	Lâstik çizme	larsteek cheezmeh
sandals	Sandal	sahndahl
scarf	Eşarp	ehshahrp
shirt	Gömlek	gurmlehk

shoes	Ayakkabı	ahyahkkahbı
shorts	Şort	short
skirt	Etek	ehtehk
slip	Jüpon	zhewpon
slippers	Terlik	tehrleek
socks	Çorap	chorahp
sports jacket	Spor ceket	spor jehkeht
stockings	Kadın çotabı	kahdın chorahbı
stole	Etol	ehtol
suit (man's)	Kostüm	kostewm
suit (woman's)	Tayör	tahyurr
suspenders (Am.)	Pantalon askısı	pahntahlon ahskıssı
sweater	Süveter	sewvehtehr
sweatshirt	Eşofman üstü	ehshofmahn ewstew
swimsuit	Mayo	mahyo
T-shirt	Tişort	teeshort
tennis shoes	Tenis ayakkabısı	tehneess ahyahkkahbıssı
tie	Kravat	krahvaht
tights	Külotlu çorap	kewlotloo chorahp
top coat	Pardösü	pahrdurssew
track suit	Örgü şömiziye	urrgrew shurmeezeeyeh
trousers	Pantalon	pahntahlon
tuxedo	Smokin	smokeen
twin set	Kazak-yelek takımı	kahzahk-yehlehk tahkımı
underpants (men)	Külot	kewlot
undershirt	Atlet	ahtleht
vest (Am.)	Yelek	yehlehk
vest (Br.)	Atlet	ahtleht
waistcoat	Yelek	yehlehk

belt	Kemer	kehmehr
buckle	Toka	tokah
button	Düğme	dewmeh
collar	Yaka	yahkah
cuffs	Manşet	mahnsheht
elastic	Lâstik	larsteek
hem	Baskı	bahskı
lapel	Röver	rurvehr
lining	Astar	ahstahr
pocket	Cep	jehp
ribbon	Kurdelâ	koordehlar
shoe laces	Ayakkabı bağı	ahyahkkahbı bahı
sleeve	Elbise kolu	ehlbeesseh koloo
zip (zipper)	Fermuar	fehrmooahr

Electrical appliances and accessories—Records

The voltage is generally 220 V, 50-cycle AC, though 110 V is also found, especially on the European side of Istanbul. Ask before plugging in your shaver, hair dryer or other appliance. Adapter plugs must have two round pins for use in Turkish outlets.

What's the voltage?	Voltaj kaçtır?	voltahzh kahchtır
Is it AC or DC?	Akım alternatif midir, düz müdür?	ahkım ahltehrnahteef medeer dewz mewdewr
I want a plug for this...	Bu ... için bir fiş istiyorum.	boo ... eecheen beer feesh eesteeyoroom
Do you have a battery for this?	Bu ... için pil var mı?	boo ... eecheen peel vahr mı
This is broken. Can you repair it?	Kırıldı. Tamir edebilir misiniz?	kırıldı. tahmeer ehdehbeeleer meesseeneez
When will it be ready?	Ne zaman hazır olur?	neh zahmahn hahzır oloor
I'd like a/an/some...	... istiyorum.	... eesteeyoroom
adapter	Ek kordon	ehk kordon
amplifier	Anplifikatör	ahnpleefeekahturr
battery	Pil	peel
blender	Mikser	meeksehr
clock	Saat	sart
wall clock	Duvar saati	doovahr sartee
food mixer	Mikser	meeksehr
hair dryer	Saç kurutma makinası	sahch koorootmah mahkeenahssı
iron	Ütü	ewtew
travelling iron	Seyahat için küçük ütü	sehyahhaht eecheen kewchewk ewtew
kettle	Elektrikli çaydanlık	ehlehktreeklee chahydahnlık
plug	Fiş	feesh
radio	Radyo	rahdyo
car radio	Otomobil radyosu	otomobeel rahdyossoo
portable radio	El radyosu	ehl rahdyossoo
record player	Pikap	peekahp
portable	Portatif pikap	portahteef peekahp
shaver	Traş makinası	trash mahkeenahssı
speakers	Oparlör	ohpahrlewr
tape recorder	Teyp	tayp
cassette	Kaset teypi	kahsseht taypee
portable	Portatif teyp	portahteef tayp

120

SHOPPING GUIDE

television	**Televizyon**	tehlehveezyon
colour	**Renkli televizyon**	rehnklee tehlehveezyon
portable	**Portatif televizyon**	portahteef tehlehveezyon
toaster	**Ekmek kızartacağı**	ehkmehk kızahrtahjahı
transformer	**Transformatör**	trahnsfohrmahturr
Turkish coffee maker	**Cezve**	jehzhveh

Record shop

Do you have any records by...?	**...'nın plâğı var mı?**	...nın plahı vahr mı
Do you have ...'s latest album?	**...'nın son albümü var mı?**	...nın son ahlbewmew vahr mı
Can I listen to this record?	**Bu plağı dinleyebilir miyim?**	boo plahı deenlehyehbeeleer meeyeem
I'd like a cassette.	**Kaset istiyorum.**	kahsseht eesteeyoroom
I want a new needle.	**Yeni bir iğne istiyorum.**	yehnee beer eeneh eesteeyoroom

L.P.	L.P.	long play
33/45 rpm	33/45 tur	ohtoozewch/kıhrkbesh
mono/stereo	mono/stereo	mohnoh/stehrehoh

chamber music	**oda müziği**	odah mewzeeee
classical music	**klasik müzik**	klahseek mewzeek
folk music	**halk müziği**	hahlk mewzeeee
instrumental music	**enstrümantal müzik**	ehnstrewmahntahl mewzeek
jazz	**caz**	jahz
light music	**hafif müzik**	hahfeef mewzeek
orchestral music	**orkestra müziği**	orkehstrah mewzeeee
pop music	**pop müzik**	pop mewzeek

Here are the names of a few popular recording artists known throughout Turkey:

Behiye Aksoy	**Tanju Okan**
Fikret Kızılok	**Ajda Pekkan**
Nilüfer Koçyiğit	**Emel Sayın**
Bariş Manço	**Şenay**
Zeki Müren	**Gönül Yazar**

Hairdressing—At the barber's

I'm in a hurry.	**Acelem var.**	ahjehlehm vahr
I want a haircut, please.	**Saçlarımı kestirmek istiyorum.**	sahchlahrımı kehsteermehk eesteeyoroom
I'd like a shave.	**Sakal traşı olmak istiyorum.**	sahkahl trahshı olmahk eesteeyoroom
Don't cut it too short.	**Çok kısa kesmeyin.**	chok kıssah kehsmehyeen
Scissors only, please.	**Yanlız makas kullanın, lütfen.**	yahnlız mahkahss koollahnın lewtfehn
A razor cut, please.	**Ustura ile saç traşı olmak istiyorum.**	oostoorah eeleh sahch trahshı olmahk eesteeyoroom
Don't use the clippers.	**Saç kesme makinası kullanmayın.**	sahch kehsmeh mahkeenahssı koollahnmahyın
Just a trim, please.	**Sadece tarayın.**	sahdehjeh tahrahyın
That's enough off.	**Böyle yeteri kadar kısa.**	buryleh yehtehree kahdahr kıssah
A little more off the...	**Biraz daha ...**	beerahz dahhah
back	**arkadan**	ahrkahdahn
neck	**enseden**	ehnsehdehn
sides	**kenarlardan**	kehnahrlahrdahn
top	**üstünden**	ewstewndehn
Please don't use any oil.	**Briyantin sürmeyin.**	breeyahnteen sewrmehyeen
Would you please trim my...?	**... tarar mısınız?**	... tahrahr mıssınız
beard	**Sakalımı**	sahkahlımı
moustache	**Bıyığımı**	bıyımı
sideboards (sideburns)	**Favorilerimi**	fahvoreelehreemee
Thank you. That's fine.	**Teşekkür ederim. Gayet iyi.**	tehshehkkewr ehdehreem. gahyeht eeyee
How much do I owe you?	**Borcum ne kadar?**	borjoom neh kahdahr
This is for you.	**Bu sizin için.**	boo seezeen eecheen

Giving 10% would be a fair tip.

Ladies' hairdressing

Is there a hairdresser's in the hotel?	Otelde kuaför salonu var mı?	otehldeh kooahfurr sahlonoo vahr mı
Can I make an appointment for some-time on Thursday?	Perşembe gününe bir randevu alabilir miyim?	pehrshehmbeh gᵛewnewneh beer rahndehvoo ahlahbeeleer meeyeem
I'd like it cut and shaped.	Mizanpli yaptırmak istiyorum.	meezahnplee yahptırmahk eesteeyoroom

with a fringe (bangs)	kâhkül	karhkewl
a razor cut	ustura ile kesme	oostoorah eeleh kehsmeh
a re-style	yeni bir saç şekli	yehnee beer sahch shehklee
with ringlets	bukleli	booklehlee
with waves	dalgalı	dahlgahlı
in a bun	topuz	topooz

I want a...	... istiyorum.	... eesteeyoroom
bleach	Dekoloran	dehkolorahn
colour rinse	Şampuan boya	shahmpooahn boyah
dye	Boya	boyah
permanent	Permanan	pehrmahnahn
shampoo and set	Misanpli	meezahnplee
tint	Hafif boyama	hahfeef boyahmah
touch up	Tarama	tahrahmah
the same colour	Aynı rengi	ahynı rehngᵛee
a darker colour	Daha koyu bir ton	dahhah koyoo beer ton
a lighter colour	Daha açık bir ton	dahhah ahchık beer ton
auburn / blond / brunette	Kumral / Sarışın / Esmer	koomrahl / sahrıshın / ehsmehr
Do you have a colour chart?	Renk kataloğunuz var mı?	rehnk kahtahlooonooz vahr mı
I don't want any hairspray.	Sprey istemiyorum.	spray eestehmeeyoroom
I want a...	... istiyorum.	... eesteeyoroom
manicure / pedicure	Manikür / Pedikür	mahneekewr / pehdeekewr
face-pack	Güzellik maskesi	gᵛewzehlleek mahskehsee

Tipping: 10%

Jeweller's—Watchmaker's

Can you repair this watch?	Bu saati tamir edebilir misiniz?	boo sartı tahmeer ehdeh-beeleer meesseeneez
The...is broken.	... kırılmış.	... kırılmısh
glass/spring strap/winder	Camı/Yayı Kayışı/Pimi	jahmı/yayhı kahyıshı/peemee
I want this watch cleaned.	Bu saati temiz-letmek istiyorum.	boo sartı tehmeez-lehtmehk eesteeyoroom
When will it be ready?	Ne zaman hazır olur?	neh zahmahn hahzır oloor
Could I please see that?	Şunu görebilir miyim, lütfen?	shoonoo gurrehbeeleer meeyeem lewtfehn
I'm just looking around.	Şöyle bir bakıyorum.	shurleh beer bahkıyoroom
I want a small present for...	... için küçük bir hediye istiyorum.	... eecheen kewchewk beer hehdeeyeh eesteeyoroom
I don't want anything too expensive.	Fazla pahalı birşey istemiyorum.	fahzlah pahhahlı beershay eesteemeeyoroom
I want something...	... birşey istiyorum.	... beershay eesteeyoroom
better	Daha iyi	dahhah eeyee
cheaper	Daha ucuz	dahhah oojooz
simpler	Daha basit	dahhah bahseet
Do you have anything in gold?	Altından birşeyiniz var mı?	ahltındahn beershayeeneez vahr mı
Is this real silver?	Bu hakiki gümüş müdür?	boo hahkeekee g{sup}v{/sup}ewmewsh mewdewr

If it's made of gold, ask:

How many carats is this?	Kaç ayardır?	kahch ahyahrdır

When you go to a jeweller's, you've probably got some idea of what you want beforehand. Find out what the article is made of and then look up its name in Turkish in the following lists.

SHOPPING GUIDE

What's it made of?

alabaster	**sumermeri**	soomehrmehree
amber	**kehlibar**	kehhleebahr
amethyst	**ametist**	ahmehteest
brass	**pirinç**	peereench
chromium	**krom**	krom
copper	**bakır**	bahkır
coral	**mercan**	mehrjahn
crystal	**kristal**	kreestahl
cut glass	**kesme cam**	kehsmeh jahm
diamond	**elmas**	ehlmahss
ebony	**abanoz**	ahbahnoz
emerald	**zümrüt**	zewmrewt
enamel	**mine**	meeneh
glass	**cam**	jahm
gold	**altın**	ahltın
gold plate	**altın kaplama**	ahltın kahplahmah
ivory	**fil dişi**	feel deeshee
jade	**yeşim taşı**	yehsheem tahshı
onyx	**damarlı akik**	dahmahrlı ahkeek
pearl	**inci**	eenjee
pewter	**kurşunlu kalay**	koorshoonloo kahlahy
platinum	**platin**	plahteen
ruby	**yâkut**	yarkoot
sapphire	**safir**	sahfeer
silver	**gümüş**	gᵛewmewsh
silver plate	**gümüş kaplama**	gᵛewmewsh kahplahmah
stainless steel	**paslanmaz çelik**	pahslahnmahz chehleek
topaz	**topaz**	topahz
turquoise	**firuze taşı**	feeroozeh tahshı

What is it?

I'd like a/an/some...	... istiyorum.	... eesteeyoroom
beads	**Boncuk**	bonjook
bracelet	**Bilezik**	beelehzeek
charm bracelet	**Uğur bileziği**	oooor beelehzeeee
brooch	**Broş**	brosh
chain	**Zincir**	zeenjeer
charm	**Muska**	mooskah
cigarette case	**Sigara tabakası**	seegahrah tahbahkahssı
cigarette lighter	**Çakmak**	chahkmahk

SHOPPING GUIDE

clock	Saat	sart
alarm clock	Çalar saat	chahlahr sart
travelling clock	Seyahat için çalar saat	sehyahhaht eecheen chahlahr sart
cross	Haç	hahch
cuff-links	Kol düğmesi	kol dewmehssee
cutlery	Gümüş yemek takımı	gᵛewmewsh yehmehk tahkımı
earrings	Küpe	kewpeh
jewel box	Mücevher kutusu	mewjehvhehr kootoossoo
manicure set	Manikür takımı	mahneekewr tahkımı
necklace	Kolye	kolyeh
pendant	Gerdanlık	gᵛehrdahnlık
pin	İğne	eeneh
powder compact	Pudriyer	poodreeyehr
ring	Yüzük	yewzewk
engagement ring	Nişan yüzüğü	neeshahn yewzewew
puzzle ring	Bilmece yüzüğü	beelmehjeh yewzewew
signet ring	Şövalye yüzük	shurvahlyeh yewzewk
wedding ring	Alyans	ahlyahnss
shishkebob skewers	Şiş	sheesh
silverware	Gümüş eşya	gᵛewmewsh ehshyah
strap	Bilezik	beelehzeek
leather strap	Saat kayışı	sart kahyıshı
tie clip	Kravat iğnesi	krahvaht eenehssee
vanity case	Makyaj çantası	mahkyahzh chahntahssı
watch	Kol saati	kol sartee
watchband	Saat bileziği	sart beelehzeeee
pocket watch	Cep saati	jehp sartee
with a second hand	Saniyeli	sahneeyehlee
wristwatch	Bilezik saat	beelehzeek sart

Laundry—Dry cleaning

If your hotel doesn't have its own laundry or dry cleaning service, ask the porter:

Where's the nearest laundry/dry cleaner's?	**En yakın çamaşırcı/ kuru temizleyici nerededir?**	ehn yah**kın** chah**mahshırjı**/ **kooroo** teh**meez**lehyeejee neh**reh**deh**deer**
I want these clothes...	**Bu elbiseleri ... istiyorum.**	boo ehl**beessehleh**ree ... ees**tee**yoroom
cleaned	**temizletmek**	teh**meez**leht**mehk**
ironed/pressed	**ütületmek**	ew**tew**leht**mehk**
washed	**yıkatmak**	yı**kaht**mahk
When will it be ready?	**Ne zaman hazır olur?**	neh zah**mahn** hahzır **oloor**
I need it...	**... lâzım.**	... lar**zım**
today	**Bugün**	boog**y**ewn
tonight	**Bu gece**	boog**y**eh**jeh**
tomorrow	**Yarına**	yahrınah
before Friday	**Cumadan önce**	joo**mah**dahn urn**jeh**
Can you...this?	**Bunu ... misiniz?**	boo**noo** ... mee**sseeneez**
mend	**örebilir**	ur**reh**bee**leer**
patch	**yamalayabilir**	yah**mah**lah**yah**bee**leer**
stitch	**dikebilir**	dee**keh**bee**leer**
Can you sew on this button?	**Bu düğmeyi dikebilir misiniz?**	boo dew**meh**ee dee**keh**-bee**leer** mee**sseeneez**
Can you get this stain out?	**Bu lekeyi çıkarabilir misiniz?**	boo leh**keh**yee chı**kah**rah-bee**leer** mee**sseeneez**
Can this be invisibly mended?	**Bunu göze batmayacak şekilde örebilir misiniz?**	boo**noo** gur**zeh** baht**mah**-yah**jahk** sheh**keel**deh **urreh**bee**leer** mee**sseeneez**
This isn't mine.	**Bu benimki değil.**	boo beh**neem**kee deh**eel**
There's one piece missing.	**Bir parça eksik.**	beer pahr**chah** ehk**seek**
There's a hole in this.	**Bunda bir delik var.**	boon**dah** beer deh**leek** vahr
Is my laundry ready?	**Çamaşırlarım hazır mı?**	chah**mahshır**lahrım hahzır **mı**

Photography—Cameras

A wide variety of film is available in major cities at prices a bit higher than at home. Colour processing is done in Ankara and Istanbul.

I want an inexpensive camera.	**Ucuz bir fotoğraf makinası istiyorum.**	oojooz beer fotorahf mahkeenahssı eesteeyoroom

Film

I'd like a/some...	**... istiyorum.**	... eesteeyoroom
film for this camera	**Bu makina için filim**	boo mahkeenah eecheen feeleem
120 film	**120 lik filim**	yewzyeermee-leek feeleem
126 film	**126 lık filim**	yewzyeermeeahltıh-lık feeleem
127 film	**127 lik filim**	yewzyeermeeyehdee-leek feeleem
135 film	**135 lik filim**	yewzohtoozbehsh-leek feeleem
620 film	**620 lik filim**	ahltıhyewzyeermee-leek feeleem
standard 8-mm	**8 mm. lik standart filim**	sehkeez meeleemehtrehleek stahndahrt feeleem
super 8-mm	**8 mm. lik süper filim**	sehkeez meeleemehtrehleek sewpehr feeleem
single 8-mm	**8 mm. lik normal filim**	sehkeez meeleemehtrehleek normahl feeleem
16-mm film	**16 mm. lik filim**	ohnahltıh meeleemehtrehleek feeleem
20/36 exposures	**20/36 pozluk**	yeermee/ohtookahltıh pozlook
this ASA/DIN number	**ASA'sı/DIN'i bu**	ahssah ssı/dın ee boo
fast/fine grain	**Normal/Hassas filim**	normahl/hahssahss feeleem
black and white	**siyah-beyaz**	seeyahh-behyahz
colour negative	**renkli**	rehnklee
colour slide	**renkli slayt**	rehnklee slahyt
artificial light type	**sûnî ışıklandırma**	soonee ıshıklahndırmah
daylight type (outdoor)	**gün ışığı**	gᵘewn ıshıı
Does the price include developing?	**Filimlerin banyo parası fiata dahil midir?**	feeleemlehreen bahnyo pahrahsı feeahtah dahheel meedeer

FOR NUMBERS, see page 175

Processing

How much do you charge for developing/printing?	**Banyo için/Basmaya ne alıyorsunuz?**	bahnyo eecheen / bahsmahyah neh ahlıyorsoonooz
I want...prints of each negative.	**Her negatiften ... tane basılmasını istiyorum.**	hehr nehgahteeftehn... tahneh bahssılmahssını eesteeyoroom
with a glossy / mat finish	**parlak/mat baskı**	pahrlahk/maht bahskı
Will you please enlarge this?	**Bunu büyültebilir misiniz, lütfen?**	boonoo bewyewltehbeelee meesseeneez lewtfehn
When will it be ready?	**Ne zaman hazır olur?**	neh zahmahn hahzır oloor

Accessories

I want a/an/some...	**... istiyorum.**	... eesteeyoroom
flash bulbs	**Flaş lâmbası**	flahsh larmbahssı
flash cubes	**Küp flaş**	kewp flahsh
for black and white	**Siyah-beyaz için**	seeyahh-behyahz eechee
for colour	**Renkli fotoğraf için**	rehnklee fotorahf eecheen
filter	**Filtre**	feeltreh
red/yellow	**kırmızı/sarı**	kırmızı/sahrı
ultra-violet	**ültraviyole**	ewltrahveeyoleh
lens cap	**Objektif kapağı**	obzhehkteef kahpahı

Broken

This camera doesn't work. Can you repair it?	**Bu fotoğraf makinası çalışmıyor. Tamir edebilir misiniz?**	boo fotorahf mahkeenahss chahlıshmıyor. tahmeer ehdehbeeleer meesseeneez
The film is jammed.	**Filim sıkıştı.**	feeleem sıkıshtıh
There's something wrong with the...	**... ârızalı**	... arrızahlı
exposure counter	**Pozometre sayacı**	pozomehtreh sahyahjı
film winder	**Filim çevirme düğmesi**	feeleem chehveermeh dewmehssee
lightmeter	**Pozometre**	pozomehtreh
rangefinder	**Mesafe ayarı**	mehssahfeh ahyahrı
shutter	**Diyafram**	deeyahfrahm

Provisions

Here's a basic list of food and drink that you might want on a picnic or for the occasional meal at home:

I'd like a/an/ some..., please.	... istiyorum, lütfen.	... eesteeyoroom lewt**fehn**
apples	**Elma**	ehlmah
bananas	**Muz**	mooz
biscuits (Br.)	**Bisküvi**	beeskewvee
bread	**Ekmek**	ehkmehk
butter	**Tereyağı**	tehrehyahı
cakes	**Pasta**	pahstah
candy	**Şekerleme**	shehkehrlehmeh
cheese	**Peynir**	payneer
chocolate	**Çikolata**	cheekolahtah
coffee	**Kahve**	kahhveh
cold cuts	**Şarküteri**	shahrkewtehree
cookies	**Bisküvi**	beeskewvee
cooking fat	**Sade yağ**	sahdeh yah
crackers	**Bisküvi**	beeskewvee
cream	**Kaymak-Krema**	kahymahk-krehmah
crisps	**Cips**	jeepss
cucumbers	**Salatalık**	sahlahtahlık
eggs	**Yumurta**	yoomoortah
flour	**Un**	oon
frankfurters	**Sosis**	sosseess
ham	**Jambon**	zhahmbon
hamburgers	**Hamburger**	hahmboorg**y**ehr
ice-cream	**Dondurma**	dondoormah
lemonade	**Limonata**	leemonahtah
lemons	**Limon**	leemon
lettuce	**Lâhana**	larhahnah
luncheon meat	**Değişik salamlar**	deheesheek sahlahmlahr
milk	**Süt**	sewt
mustard	**Hardal**	hahrdahl
oranges	**Portakal**	portahkahl
pâté	**Kaz ciğeri ezmesi**	kahz jeeehree ehzmehssee
pepper	**Karabiber**	kahrahbeebehr
pickles	**Turşu**	toorshoo
potato chips	**Cips**	jeeps
potatoes	**Patates**	pahtahtehss
rolls	**Sandviç ekmeği**	sahnd**v**eech ehkmehee
salad	**Salata**	sahlahtah
salami	**Macar salamı**	mahjahr sahlahmıh
salt	**Tuz**	tooz

sandwiches	**Sandviç**	sahndveech
sausages	**Domuz sucuğu**	domooz soojoooo
spaghetti	**Spagetti**	spahgrehtee
sugar	**Şeker**	shehkehr
sweets	**Bonbon**	bonbon
tea	**Çay**	chahy
tomatoes	**Domates**	domahtehss

And don't forget…

a bottle opener	**Şişe açacağı**	sheesheh ahchahjahı
a corkscrew	**Tirbüşon**	teerbewshon
matches	**Kibrit**	keebreet
(paper) napkins	**Kâğıt peçete**	kart pehchehteh
a tin (can) opener	**Konserve açacağı**	konsehrveh ahchahjahı

PROVISIONS

Weights and measures
1 kilogram or kilo (kg) = 1000 grams (g)

| 100 g = 3.5 oz. | ½ kg = 1.1 lb. |
| 200 g = 7.0 oz. | 1 kg = 2.2 lb. |

1 oz. = 28.35 g
1 lb. = 453.60 g

1 litre (l) = 0.88 imp. quarts = 1.06 U.S. quarts

| 1 imp. quart = 1.14 l | 1 U.S. quart = 0.95 l |
| 1 imp. gallon = 4.55 l | 1 U.S. gallon = 3.8 l |

barrel	**fıçı**	fıchı
box	**kutu**	kootoo
can	**konserve kutusu**	konsehrveh kootoossoo
carton	**karton kutu**	kahrton kootoo
crate	**küfe**	kewfeh
jar	**kavanoz**	kahvahnoz
packet	**paket**	pahkeht
tin	**konserve kutusu**	konsehrveh kootoossoo
tube	**tüp**	tewp

Souvenirs

The bazaar—covering several acres with thousands of stalls—is doubtless the most fascinating place to shop for souvenir items. There you'll have to match your skill at haggling with the vendor. Large cities have quarters with markets specializing only in certain wares. Sometimes you may run across an auction. For the more conventional traveller, there are a wide variety of shops and stores where the sales price is generally fixed.

Antiques are extremely rare and should only be bought in well-established shops. Don't forget that the government regulates antique export, and a permit may be required.

Silk, suede, sheepskin and leather are of exceptional quality. The prized Turkish carpets are those woven in Bunyan, Isparta, Usak, Kula, Gordes, Milas, Bergama, Herek, Sivas and Ladik.

Ornaments made of gold, silver, ceramic, alabaster, copper and brass are highly valued. Pipe smokers will want to examine the choice of good meerschaums.

Here are the names in Turkish of a few of the things you may have on your shopping list:

carpet	**halı**	hahlı
hooka pipe	**hazneli pipo**	hahznehlee peepo
meerschaum pipe	**lületaşı pipo**	lewlehtahshı peepo
prayer beads	**tesbih**	tehsbeeh
prayer rug	**seccâde**	sehjjardeh
puzzle ring	**bilmece yüzüğü**	beelmehjeh yewzewew
samovar	**semaver**	sehmahvehr
shishkebob skewers	**şiş**	sheesh
sugar sweet	**helva**	hehlvah
Turkish delight	**lokum**	lokoom
Turkish slippers	**terlik**	tehrleek

Tobacconist's

Turkish tobacco is widely exported and blended to produce well-known cigarettes at home and abroad. You may want to sample some of the local cigarettes which can even be bought individually from street vendors. As in America and Britain, cigarettes are generally referred to by their brand names like *Efes, Samsun* and *Yeni Harman*. Foreign cigarettes are heavily taxed and therefore very expensive.

Give me a/an/ some..., please.	Bana ... verin, lütfen.	bahnah ... vehreen lewtfehn
box of cigars	bir kutu puro	beer kootoo pooro
cigar	bir puro	beer pooro
some cigars	birkaç puro	beerkahch pooro
cigarette case	bir sigara tabakası	beer seegahrah tahbahkahssı
cigarette holder	bir ağızlık	beer ahızlık
cigarette lighter	bir çakmak	beer chahkmahk
flints	çakmak taşı	chahkmahk tahshı
lighter	çakmak	chahkmahk
lighter fluid	çakmak benzini	chahkmahk behnzeenee
lighter gas	çakmak gazı	chahkmahk gahzı
refill for a lighter	çakmak için refil	chahkmahk eecheen rehfeel
matches	kibrit	keebreet
packet of cigarettes	bir paket sigara	beer pahkeht seegahrah
packet of...	bir paket...	beer pahkeht
pipe	bir pipo	beer peepo
meerschaum pipe	lületaşı pipo	lewlehtahshı peepo
pipe cleaners	pipo temizleme	peepo tehmeezlehmeh
pipe rack	çubuğu	chooboooo
pipe tobacco	pipo kutusu	peepo kootoossoo
pipe tool	pipo tütünü	peepo tewtewnew
snuff	pipo maşası	peepo mahshahssı
tobacco pouch	enfiye	ehnfeeyeh
wick	bir tütün kesesi	beer tewtewn kehssehssee
	fitil	feeteel

filter tipped	filtreli	feeltrehlee
without filter	filtresiz	feeltrehsseez
king-size	uzun	oozoon

Do you have any…?	… var mı?	… vahr mı
American cigarettes	Amerikan sigarası	ahmehreekahn seegahrahssı
English cigarettes	İngiliz sigarası	eengveeleez seegahrahssı
Turkish cigarettes	Türk sigarası	tewrk seegahrahssı
menthol cigarettes	Mentollü sigara	mehntollew seegahrah
I'll take two packets.	İki paket istiyorum.	eekee pahkeht eesteeyoroom
I'd like a carton.	Bir karton istiyorum.	beer kahrton eesteeyoroom

While we're on the subject of cigarettes, suppose you want to offer somebody one?

Would you like a cigarette?	Sigara ister misiniz?	seegahrah eestehr meesseeneez
Have one of mine.	Benimkilerden bir tane almaz mısınız?	behneemkeelehrdehn beer tahneh ahlmahz mıssınız
Try one of these.	Bunlardan bir tane alsanız?	boonlahrdahn beer tahneh ahlsahnız
They're very mild.	Bunlar çok hafif.	boonlahr chok hahfeef
They're a bit strong.	Bunlar biraz sert.	boonlahr beerahz sehrt

And if somebody offers you one?

Thank you.	Teşekkür ederim.	tehshehkkewr ehdehreem
No, thanks.	Hayır, teşekkür ederim.	hahyır tehshehkkewr ehdehreem
I don't smoke.	Sigara içmiyorum.	seegahrah eechmeeyoroom
I've given it up.	Sigarayı bıraktım.	seegahrahyı bırahktım

Your money: banks—currency

At larger banks there's sure to be someone who speaks English. At most tourist resorts you'll find small currency exchanges *(kambiyo)*, especially during the summer season. Traveller's cheques should be changed in large cities and resorts as you may run into difficulty getting them changed in remote areas.

According to government regulations, travellers entering Turkey can bring in only 1,000 liras in cash into the country. To avoid possible difficulties and embarrassment, you'd be well advised to make foreign-exchange transactions only at banking institutions—not from men on the street.

Hours

Banking hours are from Monday to Friday from 8.30 a.m. to noon and 1.30 to 5 p.m. At Istanbul's Yesilkoy Airport the currency exchange remains open to accommodate incoming passengers.

Monetary unit

The basic unit of the Turkish monetary system is the lira (sometimes referred to in English as a pound) which is divided into 100 *kuruş*. The abbreviation for lira is TL and that for *kuruş* is kr.

Coins	Notes
50 kuruş	5 liras
1 lira	10 liras
2½ liras	20 liras
5 liras	50 liras
	100 liras
	500 liras
	1,000 liras

135

Before going

Where's the nearest bank/currency-exchange office?	En yakın banka/kambiyo bürosu nerededir?	ehn yahkın bahnkah/kahmbeeyo bewrossoo nehrehdehdeer
Where can I cash a traveller's cheque (check)?	Nerede seyahat çeki bozdurabilirim?	nehrehdeh sehyahhaht chehkee bozdoorahbeeleereem
Where's the İş Bank?	İş bankası nerededir?	eesh bahnkahssı nehrehdehdeer

Inside

I want to change some dollars.	Dolar bozdurmak istiyorum.	dolahr bozdoormahk eesteeyoroom
I'd like to change some pounds.	Sterlin bozdurmak istiyorum.	stehrleen bozdoormahk eesteeyoroom
What's the exchange rate?	Resmi kur nedir?	rehsmee koor nehdeer
What rate of commission do you charge?	Ne kadar komisyon alıyorsunuz?	neh kahdahr komeessyon ahlıyorsoonooz
Can you cash a personal cheque?	Şahsî banka çeki bozuyor musunuz?	shahhsee bahnkah chehkee bozooyor moossoonooz
How long will it take to clear?	Çekin karşılığını ne kadar zaman içinde ödeyebilirsiniz?	chehkeen kahrshılını neh kahdahr zahmahn eecheendeh urdehyehbeeleerseeneez
Can you wire my bank in Paris?	Paris'e, bankama telgraf çekebilir misiniz?	pahreesseh bahnkahmah tehlgrahf chehkehbeeleer meesseeneez
I have...	... var.	... vahr
a letter of credit	İtibar mektubum	eeteebahr mehktooboom
an introduction from...	...'den tavsiye mektubum	...dehn tahvseeyeh mehktooboom
a credit card	Kredi kartım	krehdee kahrtım
I'm expecting some money from London. Has it arrived yet?	Londra'dan para bekliyorum. Geldi mi acaba?	londrahdahn pahrah behkleeyoroom. grehldee mee ahjahbah
Please give me...100-lira notes (bills) and some small change.	... tane 100 lük ile bozukluk verin lütfen.	...tahneh 100 lewk eeleh bozooklook vehreen lewtfehn

BANK

| Give me ... large notes and the rest in small notes. | ... tane büyük, kalan için de küçük banknotlar verin. | ... tahneh bewyewk kahlahn eecheen deh kewchewk bahnknotlahr vehreen |
| Could you please check that again? | Tekrar kontrol eder misiniz, lütfen? | tehkrahr kontrol ehdehr meesseeneez lewtfehn |

Depositing

I want to credit this to my account.	Bunu hesabıma yatırmak istiyorum.	boonoo hehssahbımah yahtırmahk eesteeyoroom
I want to credit this to Mr...'s account.	Bunu ... Bey'in hesabına yatırmak istiyorum.	boonoo ... bayeen hehssahbınah yahtırmahk eesteeyoroom
Where should I sign?	Nereyi imzalaman lâzım?	nehrehyee eemzahlahmahm larzım

Currency converter

In a world of fluctuating exchange rates, we can offer no more than this do-it-yourself chart. You can get a card showing current exchange rates from banks, travel agents and tourist offices. Why not fill in this chart, too, for handy reference?

Tl	£	$
25 kuruş		
50 kuruş		
1 lira		
2½ liras		
5 liras		
10 liras		
20 liras		
50 liras		
100 liras		
500 liras		
1000 liras		

FOR NUMBERS, see page 175

At the post office

The post, telephone and telegraph office is indicated by the letters PTT. Hours may vary but are generally from 8.30 a.m. to noon and from 1 to 5.30 p.m. Major cities usually have at least one post office open after hours. Mailboxes are painted yellow.

Where's the nearest post office?	**En yakın postahane nerededir?**	ehn yahkın postahhahneh nehrehdehdeer
What time does the post office open/close?	**Postahane saat kaçta açılır/kaçta kapanır?**	postahhahneh sart kahchtah ahchılır/kahchtah kahpahnır
What window do I go to for stamps?	**Pul için hangi gişeye gitmem lâzım?**	pool eecheen hahngⁱee gⁱeeshehyeh gⁱeetmehm larzım
At which counter can I cash an international money order?	**Yabancı ülkeden gelen bir havaleyi hangi gişeden alabilirim?**	yahbahnjı ewlkehdehn gⁱehlehn beer hahvahlehyee hahngⁱee gⁱeeshehdehn ahlahbeeleereem
I want some stamps, please.	**Birkaç pul istiyorum, lütfen.**	beerkahch pool eesteeyoroom lewtfehn
I want ... 175-kuruş stamps and ... 400-kuruş stamps.	**... tane 175 kuruşluk, ... tane 400 kuruşluk pul istiyorum.**	... tahneh 175 koorooshlook ... tahneh 400 koorooshlook pool eesteeyoroom

Note: Stamps in denominations of more than 100 kuruş are still referred to in *kuruş* rather than liras. Thus you'd ask for a 400-*kuruş* stamp, not a 4-lira stamp.

What's the postage for a letter to London?	**Londra'ya mektup tarifesi nedir?**	londrahyah mehktoop tahreefehssee nehdeer
What's the postage for a postcard to Los Angeles?	**Los Angeles'e kart-postal kaça gider?**	loss ehnjehlehsseh kahrtpostahl kahchah gⁱeedehr
Do all letters go airmail?	**Bütün mektuplar uçakla mı gider?**	bewtewn mehktooplahr oochahklah mı gⁱeedehr
I want to send this parcel.	**Bu koliyi göndermek istiyorum.**	boo koleeyee gurndehrmehk eesteeyoroom

Do I need to fill in a customs declaration?	Gümrük deklarasyonu formüleri doldurmam lâzım mı?	gewmrewk dehklahrahssyonoo formewlehree doldoormahm larzım mı
Where's the mailbox?	Posta kutusu nerede acaba?	postah kootoossoo nehrehdeh ahjahbah
I want to send this by...	Bunu...göndermek istiyorum.	boonoo ... gurndehrmehk eesteeyoroom
airmail	uçakla	oochahklah
express (special delivery)	ekspres	ehksprehss
registered mail	taahhütlü	tahahewtlew
Where's the poste restante (general delivery)?	Post restant neFnededir?	post rehstahnt nehrehdehdeer
Is there any mail for me? My name is...	Bana posta var mı acaba? Adım...	bahnah postah vahr mı ahjahbah? ahdım
Here's my passport.	İşte pasaportum.	eeshteh pahssahportoom

PUL	STAMPS	
KOLİ	PARCELS	
HAVALE	MONEY ORDERS	

Telegrams

Where's the nearest telegraph office?	En yakın postahane nerededir?	ehn yahkın postahhahneh nehrehdehdeer
I want to send a telegram. May I please have a form?	Telgraf yollamak istiyorum. Bir formüler verir misiniz, lütfen?	tehlgrahf yollahmahk eesteeyoroom. beer formewlehr vehreer meesseeneez lewtfehn
How much is it per word?	Kelimesi kaçadır?	kehleemehssee kahchahdır
How long will a cable to Boston take?	Boston'a telgraf ne kadar zamanda gider?	bostonah tehlgrahf neh kahdahr zahmahndah g^yeedehr
I'd like to reverse the charges.	Ödemeli istiyorum.	urdehmehlee eesteeyoroom

Telephoning

The telephone system is generally good. Direct dialling isn't possible. After 8 p.m. or on Sundays there are reduced rates. Drop a 1-lira coin into a pay phone for a local call; post-offices often have pay phones which require a token that you can buy at a counter.

General

Where's the telephone?	**Telefon nerededir?**	tehlehfon nehrehdehdeer
Where's the nearest telephone booth?	**En yakın telefon kulübesi nerededir?**	ehn yahkın tehlehfon koolewbehssee nehrehdehdeer
I'd like a token to make a phone call.	**Bir telefon jötonu istiyorum.**	beer tehlehfon zhurtonoo eesteeyoroom
Do you have a telephone directory for Ankara?	**Ankara telefon rehberi var mı?**	ahnkahrah tehlehfon rehhbehree vahr mı
Can you help me get this number?	**Şu numarayı bulmama yardım eder misiniz?**	shoo noomahrahyı bollmahmah yahrdım ehdehr meesseeneez

Operator

Do you speak English?	**İngilizce biliyor musunuz?**	eengveeleezjeh beeleeyor moossoonooz
Good morning, I want Izmir 123456.	**Izmir'de 123456 yı istiyorum, lütfen.**	eezmeerdeh 123456 yı eesteeyoroom lewtfehn

Note: Numbers are given in pairs.

I want to place a personal (person-to-person) call.	**İhbarlı aramak istiyorum.**	eehhbahrlı ahrahmahk eesteeyoroom
I want to reverse the charges.	**Ödemeli etmek istiyorum.**	urdehmehlee ehtmehk eesteeyoroom
Will you tell me the cost of the call afterwards?	**Görüşmeden sonra ücreti söyler misiniz, lütfen?**	gurrewshmehdehn sonrah ewjrehtee surylehr meesseeneez lewtfehn

FOR NUMBERS, see page 175

Speaking

Hello. This is... speaking.	Alo, ben...	ahlo behn
I want to speak to...	... ile görüşmek istiyorum.	... eeleh gurrewshmehk eesteeyoroom
Would you put me through to...?	...i verir misiniz, lütfen.	...ı vehreer meesseeneez lewtfehn
I want extension...	... dahilî istiyorum.	... dahheelee eesteeyoroom
Is that...?	..., ile mi görüşüyorum?	... eeleh mee gurrewshewyoroom

Bad luck

Would you please try again later?	Daha sonra tekrar arar mısınız, lütfen?	dahhah sonrah tehkrahr ahrahr mıssınız lewtfehn
Operator, you gave me the wrong number.	Hanımefendi (Beyefendi*), bana yanlış numarayı bağladınız.	hahnımehfehndee (bayehfehndee) bahnah yahnlısh noomahrahyı bahlahdınız
Operator, we were cut off.	Hanımefendi (Beyefendi*), bağlantı kesildi.	hahnımehfehndee (bayehfehndee) bahlahntı kehsseeldee

Telephone alphabet

A	Adana	ahdahnah	N	Nazilli	nahzeellee
B	Balıkesir	bahlıkehsseer	O	Ordu	ordoo
C	Ceyhan	jayhahn	Ö	Ödemiş	urdehmeesh
Ç	Çorum	choroom	P	Pazar	pahzahr
D	Diyarbakır	deeyahrbahkır	Q	Quebek	kvehbehk
E	Edirne	ehdeerneh	R	Rize	reezeh
F	Fatsa	fahtsah	S	Samsun	sahmsoon
G	Giresun	gᵛeerehssoon	T	Trabzon	trahbzon
H	Hatay	hahtahy	U	Urla	oorlah
I	Irmak	ırmahk	Ü	Ünye	ewnyeh
İ	İstanbul	eestahnbool	V	Van	vahn
J	Jandarma	zhahndahrmah	W	dubel V	dooblveh
K	Kastamonu	kahstahmonoo	X	Xavier	ksahveeehr
L	Lüleburgaz	lewlehboorgahz	Y	Yozgat	yozgaht
M	Manisa	mahneessah	Z	Zonguldak	zongooldahk

* male telephone operator

Not there

When will he/she be back?	**Ne zaman dönmüş olur?**	neh zahmahn durnmewsh oloor
Will you tell him/her I called? My name's...	**Kendisini aradığımı söyler misiniz? Adım...**	kehdeesseenee ahrahdımı surylehr meesseeneez? ahdım
Would you ask him/her to call me?	**Kendisine beni aramasını söyler misiniz?**	kehdeesseeneh behnee ahrahmahssını surylehr meesseeneez
Would you please take a message?	**Lütfen not alır mısınız?**	lewtfehn not ahlır mıssınız

Charges

What was the cost of that call?	**Görüşmenin ücreti ne kadar?**	gurrewshmehneen ewjrejtee neh kahdahr
I want to pay for the call.	**Görüşmenin bedelini ödemek istiyorum.**	gurrewshmehneen behdehleenee urdehmehk eesteeyoroom

 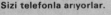

Sizi telefonla arıyorlar.	There's a telephone call for you.
Kiminle görüşüyorum, acaba?	Who's speaking?
Hangi numarayı aradınız?	What number are you calling?
Hat meşgûl.	The line's engaged (busy).
Cevap vermiyor.	There's no answer.
Yanlış numara çevirdiniz.	You've got the wrong number.
Telefon arızalı.	The phone is out of order.
Şimdilik dışarıda.	He's/She's out at the moment.

TELEPHONE

The car

Filling station

We'll start this section by considering your possible needs at a filling station. Most of them don't handle major repairs; but apart from providing you with fuel, they may be helpful in solving all kinds of minor problems.

Where's the nearest filling station?	**En yakın benzin istasyonu nerededir?**	ehn yahkın behnzeen eestahssyonoo nehrehdehdeer
I want 20 litres of petrol (gas), please.	**20 litre benzin istiyorum, lütfen.**	20 leetreh behnzeen eesteeyoroom lewtfehn
I want 30 litres of standard/premium.	**30 litre normal/ süper istiyorum.**	30 leetreh normahl / sewpehr eesteeyoroom
Give me ... liras worth of petrol (gas).	**... liralık benzin verin.**	... leerahlık behnzeen vehreen
Fill 'er up, please.	**Depoyu doldurun, lütfen.**	dehpoyoo doldooroon lewtfehn
Please check the oil and water.	**Lütfen yağı ve suyu kontrol edin.**	lewtfehn yahı veh sooyoo kontrol ehdeen
Give me 2 litres of oil.	**2 litre yağ verin, lütfen.**	2 leetreh yah vehreen lewtfehn
Fill up the battery with distilled water.	**Aküye arı su doldurun.**	ahkewyeh ahrı soo doldooroon
Check the brake fluid.	**Hidrolik yağını kontrol edin.**	heedroleek yahını kontrol ehdeen

Fluid measures					
litres	imp. gal.	U.S. gal.	litres	imp. gal.	U.S. gal.
5	1.1	1.3	30	6.6	7.8
10	2.2	2.6	35	7.7	9.1
15	3.3	3.9	40	8.8	10.4
20	4.4	5.2	45	9.9	11.7
25	5.5	6.5	50	11.0	13.0

Tire pressure is measured in Turkey in kilograms per square centimetre. The following conversion chart will make sure your tires get the treatment they deserve. Just point to the pressures required.

Tire pressure			
lb./sq. in.	kg./cm²	lb./sq. in.	kg./cm²
10	0.7	26	1.8
12	0.8	27	1.9
15	1.1	28	2.0
18	1.3	30	2.1
20	1.4	33	2.3
21	1.5	36	2.5
23	1.6	38	2.7
24	1.7	40	2.8

Would you check the tires?	**Lâstikleri kontrol eder misiniz?**	larsteeklehree kontrol ehdehr meesseeneez
1.6 front, 1.8 rear.	**Önlerin 1,6, arkaların 1,8 almasını istiyorum.**	urnlehreen 1 vergewl 6 ahrkahlahrın 1 vergewl 8 ahlmahssını eesteeyoroom
Please check the spare tire, too.	**Stepne lâstiğini de kontrol edin, lütfen.**	stehpneh larsteenee deh kontrol ehdeen lewtfehn
Can you mend this puncture (fix this flat)?	**Bu patlağı tamir eder misiniz?**	boo pahtlahı tahmeer ehdehr meesseeneez
Would you please change this tire?	**Bu lâstiği değiştirir misiniz, lütfen?**	boo larsteeee deheeshteereer meesseeneez lewtfehn
Would you clean the windscreen (windshield)?	**Ön camı temizler misiniz?**	urn jahmı tehmeezlehr meesseeneez
Have you a road map of this district?	**Bu bölgenin karayolları haritası var mı?**	boo burlgrehneen kahrahyollahrı hahreetahssı vahr mı
Where are the toilets?	**Tuvaletler nerede?**	toovahlehtlehr nehrehdeh

Asking the way—Street directions

Asking the way of someone in a language you don't know very well, if at all, can be a very frustrating experience. Especially in the large cities you might get to where you're going more quickly if you can produce a street plan and have somebody point on it the way to go. However, here are some questions you will find useful.

Excuse me.	**Affedersiniz.**	ahffehdehrseeneez
Can you tell me the way to...?	**... yolunu gösterir misiniz?**	... yoloonoo gurstehreer meesseeneez
How do I get to...?	**...'e nasıl gidebilirim?**	...'eh nahssıl gᵛeedehbeeleereem
Where does this road lead to?	**Bu yol nereye gider?**	boo yol nehrehyeh gᵛeedehr
Can you show me on this map where I am?	**Haritada nerede bulunduğumu gösterir misiniz?**	hahreetahdah nehrehdeh booloondoomoo gurstehreer meesseeneez
How far is it to... from here?	**... buradan ne kadar uzaklıktadır?**	... boorahdahn neh kahdahr oozahklıktahdır

Miles into kilometres									
1 mile = 1.609 kilometres (km.)									
miles	10	20	30	40	50	60	70	80	90	100
km.	16	32	48	64	80	97	113	129	145	161

Kilometres into miles												
1 kilometre (km.) = 0.62 miles												
km.	10	20	30	40	50	60	70	80	90	100	110	120	130
miles	6	12	19	25	31	37	44	50	56	62	68	75	81

Are we on the right road for...?	...için doğru yolda mıyız?	...eecheen dohroo yoldah mıyız
How far is the next village?	Sonraki köye ne kadar mesafe var?	sonrahkee kuryeh neh kahdahr mehssahfeh vahr
How far is it to ... from here?	Buradan ...'e kadar mesafe nedir?	boorahdahn ...eh kahdahr mehssahfeh nehdeer
Can you tell me where... is?	...'in, bana nerede olduğunu söyler misiniz?	...een bahnah nehrehdeh oldoooonoo surylehr meesseeneez
Where can I find this address?	Bu adresi nereden bulabilirim?	boo ahdrehssee nehrehdehn boolahbeeleereem
Where's this?	Nerede bu?	nehrehdeh boo
Can I park there?	Oraya park edebilir miyim?	ohrahyah pahrhk ehdehbeeleer meeyeem
Is that a one-way street?	Tek istikâmet mi?	tehk eesteekahmeht mee
What does this sign mean?	Bu işaret ne anlama gelir?	boo eeshahreht neh ahnlahmah gʲehleer

Yanlış yoldasınız.	You're on the wrong road.
Dosdoğru devam edin.	Go straight ahead.
Şurada aşağıda solda/sağda.	It's down there on the left/right.
Birinci/İkinci kavşağa kadar gidin.	Go to the first/second crossroads.
Trafik ışıklarında sola/sağa dönün.	Turn left/right at the traffic lights.

CAR—INFORMATION

In the rest of this section we'll be more closely concerned with the car itself. The section is divided into two parts:

Part A contains general advice on customs clearance and motoring in Turkey. It's essentially intended to facilitate your prior travel planning and to give you an idea of the driving conditions in the country.

Part B is the section we heartily hope every visiting motorist might find, at the end of his trip, to have been superfluous. Unfortunately even the best-laid plans of tourists and men, it must be agreed, are likely to come to grief as a telegraph pole pops up, as they will, "from nowhere" to strike a mild but sometimes crippling blow to your near-side wing, or your car suffers some kind of automotive nervous breakdown a few thousand miles from home.

Part B therefore includes a list of car parts and of things that may go wrong with them. All you have to do is to show the list to the garage mechanic and get him to point to the items and repairs required.

Part A

Customs—Documentation

To drive in Turkey you'll require the following documents:

passport
valid national driving licence (international for drivers of hired cars)
international insurance certificate (green card)

Make certain that your green card is valid in Turkey with such a clause specifically noted in the card. Third-party insurance is obligatory but you can take out a policy in Turkey for a period as short as a month. You can drive your car for up to three months in Turkey as a transit traveller, but if you think you'll be staying longer than that you should apply for a triptyque from your car insurance company before leaving home.

Here's my...	İşte...	eeshteh
driving licence	şoför ehliyetim	shofurr ehhleeyehteem
green card	yeşil kartım	yehsheel kahrtım
passport	pasaportum	pahssahportoom
I haven't anything to declare.	Deklare edecek birşeyim yok.	dehklahreh ehdehjehk beershayeem yok
I've...	... var.	... vahr
a carton of cigarettes	Bir karton sigaram	beer kahrton seegahrahm
a bottle of whisky	Bir şişe viskim	beer sheesheh veeskeem
a bottle of wine	Bir şişe şarabım	beer sheesheh shahrahbım
We're staying for...	... kalıyoruz.	... kahlıyorooz
a week	Bir hafta	beer hahftah
two weeks	İki hafta	eekee hahftah
a month	Bir ay	beer ahy

Roads

Roads in Turkey range from the sparkling new stretches of motorway (turnpike) near Istanbul to the beaten-earth country lanes in the depths of the countryside. The two most important cities of the country, Istanbul and Ankara, are linked by a very good highway and the country as a whole is crisscrossed by a network of perfectly adequate, asphalted arterial roads.

The general economic development of the country has of course been responsible for the improvement in road conditions. Thanks to the growing numbers of foreign visitors, tourist areas, both scenic and historic, have been especially favoured.

Once off the beaten track, however, you'll have to expect some slightly more adventurous roads, not so well paved and narrower, though there'll also be less traffic to worry about. In many towns further east you'll come across a good many cobbled streets.

Since service stations are often few and far between, always make sure you're not likely to run low on fuel.

You'd be advised to add an extra pinch of prudence to your driving technique and to make due allowance for the possible reactions of other road users.

A final word on the magnificent Bosphorous Bridge near Istanbul which links Europe and Asia. Opened in October 1973, in commemoration of the proclamation of the Turkish republic fifty years before, it is in itself a most impressive symbol of Turkey's position at the meeting point of these two continents.

Parking

Use your common sense when parking. The police are pretty lenient with tourists, but don't push your luck too far. You can be fined on the spot for traffic offences.

Park your vehicle in the direction of moving traffic—not against it. Obey the parking regulations which will be indicated by signs. There aren't any parking meters but there are parking areas where you may have to pay a fee. The attendant may ask you to leave the key in your car.

Excuse me. May I park here?	**Affedersiniz. Buraya park edebilir miyim?**	ahffehdehrseeneez. boorahyah pahrk ehdehbeeleer meeyeem
How long may I park here?	**Buraya ne kadar zaman için park edebilirim?**	boorahyah neh kahdahr zahmahn eecheen pahrk ehdehbeeleereem
What's the charge for parking here?	**Buranın park ücreti nedir?**	boorahnın pahrk ewjrehtee nehdeer
Do I have to leave my lights on?	**Park lâmbalarımı açık bırakmam lâzım mı?**	pahrk larmbahlahrımı ahchık bırahkmahm larzım mı
Do I have to leave my keys?	**Anahtarlarımı bırakmam lâzım mı?**	ahnahhtahrlahrımı bırahkmahm larzım mı

Turkish road signs and traffic regulations

In the main, road signs in Turkey will be readily understood
since they mostly conform to international norms. Traffic
regulations also are basically the same as you're used to at
home though you'd be advised to drive with special care until
you have acquired a feeling for the local interpretation of
these regulations. A red traffic light is of course officially a
mandatory stop signal; in the driving *mores* of the country
you may occasionally find that it seems to have something
more like the effect that a red rag has on a bull.

Don't forget to drive on the *right!*

Here are the most common Turkish-language signs you are
likely to encounter, with their English translations.

ASKERI ALAN	Military area
BOZUK SATIH	Poor surface
DEVLET HUDUDU	Border
DIKKAT	Caution
DUR	Stop
FARLARINIZI KONTROL EDİNİZ	Check your headlights
FARLARINIZI YAKINIZ	Turn on headlights
HASTANE	Hospital
HAVA ALANI	Airport
HUDUT GÜMRÜK KAPISI	Port of entry
İNŞA HALİNDEKİ YOL	Road under construction
KARAYOLLARI DİNLENME PARKI	Roadside rest area
LİMAN VE İSKELE	Seaport
MİLLİ PARK	National park
MOTORLU TAŞITLARIN GEÇEMİYECEĞİ YOL	Road unsuited to motorized vehicles
POLİS	Police
TABİAT GÜZELLİĞİ	Scenic site
TARİHİ ANIT VE ÖREN YERİ	Historical site and ruins
TEK İSTİKAMET	One-way street
TOPRAK KAYMASI	Landslide
TÜNEL	Tunnel
YANGIN TEHLİKESİ	Caution: fire
YAVAŞ	Slow

FOR INTERNATIONAL ROAD SIGNS, see pages 160–161

CAR—INFORMATION

CAR—INFORMATION

Accidents
Part B

This section is confined to immediate aid. The legal problem of responsibility and settlement can be taken care of at a later stage. Your first concern will be for the injured.

Is anyone hurt?	**Yaralı var mı?**	yahrahlı vahr mı
Don't move.	**Kımıldamayın.**	kımıldahmahyın
It's all right. Don't worry.	**Birşey yok. Merak etmeyin.**	beershay yok. mehrahk ehtmehyeen
Where's the nearest telephone?	**En yakın telefon nerede?**	ehn yahkın tehlehfon nehrehdeh
Can I use your telephone? There's been an accident.	**Telefonunuzu kullanabilir miyim? Bir kaza oldu.**	tehlehfonoonoozoo koollahnahbeeleer meeyeem? beer kahzah oldoo
Call a doctor/an ambulance quickly.	**Çabuk bir doktor/bir ambülans çağırın.**	chahbook beer doktor/beer ahmbewlahns chahrın
There are people injured.	**Yaralılar var.**	yahrahlılahr vahr
Help me get them out of the car.	**Onları arabadan çıkarmama yardım edin.**	onlahrı ahrahbahdahn chıkahrmahmah yahrdım ehdeen

Police—Exchange of information

In the event of an accident, whether anybody has been injured or not, the law requires that a police report be filed. Here are the most pressing initial expressions you'll need.

Please call the police.	**Lütfen polis çağırın.**	lewtfehn poleess chahrın
There's been an accident. It's about 2 km. from...	**Bir kaza oldu. ...'e 2 km. mesafede.**	beer kahzah oldoo. ...eh 2 keelohmehtreh mehssahfehdeh
I'm on the İstanbul–Izmit road, 25 km. from Istanbul.	**İstanbul'a 25 km. uzaklıkta, İstanbul–İzmit yolundayım.**	eestahnboolah 25 keelohmehtreh oozahklıktah eestahnbool eezmeet yoloondahyım
Here's my name and address.	**İşte adım ve adresim.**	eeshteh ahdım veh ahdrehsseem

| Would you mind acting as a witness? | **Şahitlik yapmayı kabûl ediyor musunuz?** | shahheetleek yahpmahyı kahbool ehdeeyor moossoonooz |
| I'd like an interpreter. | **Tercüman istiyorum.** | tehrjewmahn eesteeyoroom |

Remember to put out a red triangle warning sign if the car is out of action or impeding traffic.

Breakdown

1. *On the road*
   You ask where the nearest garage is.

2. *At the garage*
   You tell the mechanic what's wrong.

3. *Finding the trouble*
   He tells you what he thinks is wrong.

4. *Getting it repaired*
   You tell him to repair it and, once that lot is over, settle the account (or argue about it).

Phase 1—On the road

Where's the nearest garage?	**En yakın tamirhane nerededir?**	ehn yahkın tahmeerhahneh nehrehdehdeer
Excuse me. My car has broken down. May I use your phone?	**Affedersiniz. Arabam ârıza yaptı. Telefonunuzu kullanabilir miyim?**	ahffehdehrseeneez. ahrahbahm arrızah yahptı. tehlehfonoonoozoo koollahnahbeeleer meeyeem
What's the telephone number of the nearest garage?	**En yakın tamirhanenin telefon numarasını biliyor musunuz?**	ehn yahkın tahmeerhahnehneen tehlehfon noomahrahssını beeleeyor moossoonooz
I've had a breakdown at...	**Arabam...'de ârıza yaptı.**	ahrahbahm ...deh arrızah yahptı
Can you send a mechanic?	**Bir otomobil tamircisi gönderir misiniz?**	beer otomobeel tahmeerjeessee gurndehreer meesseeneez

| Can you send a truck to tow my car? | **Otomobilimi yedeğine alması için bir kurtarma aracı gönderir misiniz?** | otomobeeleemee yehdeheeneh ahlmassı eecheen beer koortahrmah ahrahjı gurndehreer meesseeneez |
| How long will you be? | **Ne kadar zaman sürer?** | neh kahdahr zahmahn sewrehr |

Phase 2—At the garage

Apart from a number of agency garages in the major cities, you'll find that most garage mechanics in Turkey belong to that good old solid breed that can repair anything from a wheelbarrow to a Rolls Royce. Though the odds against finding a spare carbon brush holder in the further reaches of Anatolia may seem rather long, human ingenuity has been known to master more taxing challenges. Your mechanic will very likely be able to fix you up.

Can you help me?	**Bana yardım edebilir misiniz?**	bahnah yahrdım ehdehbeeleer meesseeneez
I don't know what's wrong with it.	**Neresinin bozuk olduğunu bilmiyorum.**	nehrehsseeneen bozook oldoonoo beelmeeyoroom
I think there's something wrong with the...	**Zannedersem ... ârızalı.**	zahnnehdehrsehm ... arrızahlı

battery	**akü**	ahkew
brakes	**frenler**	frehnlehr
bulbs	**ampuller**	ahmpoollehr
carburettor	**karbüratör**	kahrbewrahturr
clutch	**debriyaj**	dehbreeyahzh
cooling system	**soğutma tertibatı**	sooootmah tehrteebahtı
cables	**kablolar**	kahblolahr
contact	**kontak**	kontahk
dimmers, dip switch	**selektör**	sehlehkturr
dynamo	**dinamo**	deenahmo
electrical system	**elektrik tertibatı**	ehlehktreek tehrteebahtı
engine	**motor**	motor
exhaust pipe	**egzost borusu**	ehgzost boroossoo
fan	**vantilatör**	vahnteelahturr
filter	**filtre**	feeltreh

fuel pump/tank	**yağ pompası/deposu**	yah pompahssı/dehpossoo
gears	**vitesler**	veetehslehr
generator	**dinamo**	deenahmo
hand brake	**el freni**	ehl frehnee
headlights	**farlar**	fahrlahr
heating	**kalorifer**	kahloreefehr
horn	**klâkson**	klarkson
ignition system	**ateşleme sistemi**	ahtehshlehmeh seestehmee
indicator	**sinyal kolu**	seenyahl koloo
lights	**lâmbalar**	larmbahlahr
brake lights	**fren lâmbaları**	frehn larmbahlahrı
rear (tail) lights	**arka lâmbalar**	ahrkah larmbahlahr
reversing (back-up) lights	**geri vites lâmbaları**	gᵛehree veetehss larmbahlahrı
lining and covering	**balata**	bahlahtah
lubrication system	**yağlama tertibatı**	yahlahmah tehrteebahtı
parking brake	**el freni**	ehl frehnee
radiator	**radyatör**	rahdyahturr
reflectors	**reflektörler**	rehflehkturrlehr
seat	**koltuk**	koltook
sliding roof	**tente**	tehnteh
sparking plugs	**bujiler**	boozheelehr
speedometer	**sürat saati**	sewraht sartee
starter	**marş motoru**	mahrsh motoroo
steering	**direksiyon**	deerehksyon
suspension	**süspansiyon**	sewspahnseeyon
(automatic) transmission	**(otomatik) vites**	otomahteek veetehss
turn signal	**sinyal**	seenyahl
wheels	**tekerlekler**	tehkehrlehklehr
wipers	**cam silecekleri**	jahm seelehjehklehree

LEFT	RIGHT		FRONT	BACK
SOL	**SAĞ**		**ÖN**	**ARKA**
(sohl)	(sah)		(urn)	(ahrkah)

It's...

bad	**Bozuk.**	bozook
blown	**Atmış.**	ahtmısh
broken	**kırık.**	kırık
burnt	**Yanmış.**	yahnmısh
cracked	**Çatlak.**	chahtlahk
defective	**Arızalı.**	ahrızahlı
disconnected	**Ayrılmış.**	ahyrılmısh

dry	Susuz.	soossooz
frozen	Donmus.	donmoosh
jammed	Sıkışmış.	sıkıshmısh
knocking	Vuruyor.	voorooyor
leaking	Kaçak yapıyor.	kahchahk yahpıyor
loose	Gevşek.	gehvshehk
misfiring	Tekliyor.	tehkleeyor
noisy	Ses yapıyor.	sehss yahpıyor
not working	Çalışmıyor.	chahlıshmıyor
overheating	Çok ısınıyor.	chok ıssınıyor
short-circuiting	Kısa devre yapıyor.	kıssah dehvreh yahpıyor
slack	Gevşek.	gehvshehk
slipping	Patinaj yapıyor.	pahteenahzh yahpıyor
stuck	Sıkışmış.	sıkıshmısh
vibrating	Titriyor.	teetreeyor
weak	Zayıf.	zahyıf
worn	Yıpranmış.	yıprahnmısh

The car won't start.	Almıyor.	ahlmıyor
It's locked and the keys are inside.	Kilitli, anahtarlar ise içinde.	keeleetlee ahnahhtahlahr eesseh eecheendeh
The fan belt is too slack.	Vantilatör lâstiği çok gevşek.	vahnteelahturr larsteeee chok gᵛehvshehk
The radiator is leaking.	Radyatör kaçak yapıyor.	rahdyahturr kahchahk yahpıyor
I want maintenance and lubrication service.	Bakım ve yağlama yapılmasını istiyorum.	bahkım veh yahlahmah yahpılmahssını eesteeyorooc
The idling needs adjusting.	Ralantı ayarı yapılması lâzım.	rahlahntee ahyahrı yahpılmahssı larzım
The clutch engages too quickly.	Debriyaj çok çabuk kavrıyor.	dehbreeyahzh chok chahbook kahvrıyor
The wipers are smearing.	Cam silecekleri kirletiyor.	jahm seelehjehklehree keerlehteeyor
The pneumatic suspension is weak.	Amortisörler yetersiz.	ahmorteessurrlehr yehtehrseez
The brakes need adjusting.	Frenlerin ayarlanması lâzım.	frehnlehreen ahyahrlahnmahssı larzım

Now that you've explained what's wrong, you'll want to know how long it'll take to repair it and make your arrangements accordingly.

How long will it take to repair?	Tamiri ne kadar sürer?	tahmeeree neh kahdahr sewrehr
How long will it take to find out what's wrong?	Ârızanın bulunması ne kadar zaman alır?	arrızahnın booloonmahssı neh kahdahr zahmahn ahlır
Suppose I come back in half an hour?	Yarım saate kadar bir uğrasam?	yahrım sarteh kahdahr beer oorahssahm
Can you give me a lift into town?	Beni şehre bırakır mısınız?	behnee shehhreh bırahkır mıssınız
Is there a place to stay nearby?	Yakında kalacak bir yer var mı?	yahkındah kahlahjahk beer yehr vahr mı
May I use your phone?	Telefonunuzu kullanabilir miyim?	tehlehfonoonoozoo koollahnahbeeleer meeyeem

Phase 3—Finding the trouble

It's up to the mechanic either to find the trouble or to repair it. All you have to do is hand him the book and point to the text in Turkish below.

İlişikteki alfabetik sırayı takip eden listeye bakıp bozuk yerleri gösterin. Müşteriniz bozukluğun nerede olduğunu bilmek istediği takdirde, diğer listede yazılı terimlere bakıp söyleyin (...kırık, kısa-devre yapmış, v.ş.). *

akü	battery
akü gözleri	battery cells
akü suyu	battery liquid
amortisör	shock-absorber
arı su	distilled water
balata	lining
benzin filtresi	petrol filter
benzin pompası	petrol pump
buji başlıkları	sparking plug leads
bujiler	sparking plugs
conta	joint
bağlantı	connection
debriyaj	clutch
debriyaj diski	clutch plate

*Please look at the following alphabetical list and point to the defective item. If your customer wants to know what's wrong with it, pick the applicable term from the next list (broken, short-circuited, etc.).

debriyaj pedalı	clutch pedal
dinamo	dynamo (generator)
direksiyon kutusu	steering box
direksiyon mili	steering column (post)
direksiyon tertibatı	steering
dişler	teeth
distribütör	distributor
distribütör kapağı	distributor leads
eksantrik mili-kamalı mil	camshaft
elektrik tertibatı	electrical system
endüksiyon bobini	ignition coil
endüvi	starter armature
enjeksiyon pompası	injection pump
filtre	filter
fren	brake
fren pabuçları	shoes
gömlek	diaphragm
gres yağı	grease
hava filtresi	air filter
havalı süspansiyon	pneumatic suspension
kablo	cable
karbüratör	carburettor
kardan contaları	universal joint
kısa rot başları	track rod ends
kömürler	brushes
kontakt	contact
krank mili	crankshaft
krank yatakları	main bearings
külbütor	stems
külbütörler	tappets
makara	rack and pinion
marş motoru	starter motor
meksefe	condenser
motor	engine
otomatik vites	automatic transmission
piston	piston
plâtinler	points
pompa	pump
pul	ring
radyatör	radiator
şaft	shaft
şamandıra	float
şanzıman	gear box
segmanlar	piston rings
selektör	dipswitch (dimmer switch)
silindir	cylinder

silindir bloku	block
silindir kapağı	cylinder head
silindir kapak contası	cylinder head gasket
soğutma tertibatı	cooling system
stabilizatör	stabilizer
supap	valve
supap yayı	valve spring
süspansiyon	suspension
su pompası	water pump
tambur	brake drum
tekerlekler	wheels
termostat	thermostat
transmisyon	transmission
üst karter	crankcase
vantilatör	fan
vantilatör kayışı	fan-belt
yağ filtresi/pompası	oil filter/pump
yağ pompası	fuel pump
yatak	bearing
yaylar	springs

Aşağıdaki liste nelerin bozuk olduğu gibi ne cins bir tamirata ihtiyaç olduğunu da belirtmektedir.*

alçak	low
aşınmış	corroded
atmış	blown
ayarlamak	to adjust
ayrılmış	disconnected
balans ayarı yapmak	to balance
balataları değiştirmek	to reline
balataları sökmek	to strip down
çabuk-seri	quick
çatlak	cracked
çok ısınıyor	overheating
değiştirmek	to replace
değiştirmek	to change
delik	puncture
doldurmak	to charge
donmuş	frozen
eğrilmiş	warped
fena	defective
gevşek	slack / loose

* The following list contains words which describe what's wrong as well as what may need to be done.

CAR—REPAIRS

gevşetmek	to loosen
kaçak yapıyor	leaking
kırık	broken
kirli	dirty
kısa	short
kısa devre yapmış	short-circuited
oynuyor	play
patinaj yapıyor	slipping
sıkışmış	stuck
sıkışmış	jammed
sıkıştırmak	to tighten
sızmak	to bleed
susuz	dry
tekliyor	misfiring
temizlemek	to clean
titriyor	vibrating
vuruyor	knocking
yanmış	burnt
yıpranmış	worn
yüksek	high
zayıf	weak

Phase 4—Getting it repaired

Have you found the trouble?	**Ârızayı buldunuz mu?**	ahrızahyı booldoonooz moo

Now that you know what's wrong, or at least have some idea, you'll want to find out…

Is that serious?	**Önemli mi?**	urnehmlee mee
Can you repair it?	**Tamir edebilir misiniz?**	tahmeer ehdehbeeleer meesseeneez
What's it going to cost?	**Kaça mâlolur?**	kahchah marloloor
Can you do it now?	**Şimdi yapabilir misiniz?**	sheemdee yahpahbeeleer meesseeneez

What if he says «no»?

Why can't you do it?	**Niçin yapamıyorsunuz?**	neecheen yahpahmıyorsoonooz
Is it essential to have that part?	**Bu parça elzem mi?**	boo pahrchah ehlzehm mee

How long is it going to take to get the spare parts ?	**Yedek parçaların gelmesi ne kadar zaman alır?**	yehdehk pahrchahlahrın g^yehlmehssee neh kahdahr zahmahn ahlır
Where is the nearest garage that can repair it ?	**Bunu tamir edebilecek en yakın garaj nerede?**	boonoo tahmeer ehdeh-beelehjehk ehn yahkın gahrahzh nehrehdeh
Can you fix it so that I can get as far as…?	**…a kadar gidebilmen için bir çaresine bakabilir misiniz?**	…ah kahdahr g^yeedeh-beelmehm eecheen beer chahrehsseeneh bahkah-beeleer meessenez

If you're really stuck, ask if you can leave the car at the garage. Contact the nearest representative of the Turkish Touring and Automobile Association—*Türk Turing Otomobil Kurumu*—or hire another car.

Settling the bill

Is everything fixed ?	**Herşeyi tamir ettiniz mi?**	hehrshayee tahmeer ehtteeneez mee
How much do I owe you?	**Borcum ne kadar?**	borjoom neh kahdahr
Will you take a traveller's cheque?	**Seyahat çeki kabul ediyor musunuz?**	sehyahhaht chehkee kahbool ehdeeyor moossoonooz
Thanks very much for your help.	**Yardımınıza çok teşekkürler.**	yahrdımınızah chok tehshehkkewrlehr
This is for you.	**Bu sizin için.**	boo seezeen eecheen

But you may feel that the workmanship is sloppy or that you're paying for work not done. Get the bill itemized. If necessary, get it translated before you pay.

I'd like to check the bill first. Will you itemize the work done?	**Önce faturayı kontrol etmek isti-yorum. Yapılan işi teferruatıyla yazar mısınız?**	urnjeh fahtoorahyı kontrol ehtmehk eesteeyoroom. yahpılahn eeshee tehfehr-rooahtıylah yahzahr mıssınız

If the garage still won't back down and you're sure you are right, get the help of a third party.

Some international road signs

No vehicles

No entry

No overtaking
(passing)

Oncoming traffic
has priority

Maximum
speed limit

No parking

Caution

Intersection

Dangerous bend
(curve)

Road narrows

Intersection
with secondary
road

Two-way traffic

Dangerous hill

Uneven road

Falling rocks

Give way (yield)

Main road,
thoroughfare

End of restriction

One-way traffic

Traffic goes
this way

Roundabout
(rotary)

Bicycles only

Pedestrians
only

Minimum speed
limit

Keep right
(left if symbol
reversed)

Parking

Hospital

Motorway
(expressway)

Motor vehicles
only

Filling station

No through road

Doctor

Frankly, how much use is a phrase book going to be to you in case of serious injury or illness? The only phrase you need in such an emergency is...

Get a doctor quickly!	**Çabuk bir doktor çağırın!**	chahbook beer doktor chahrın

But there are minor aches and pains, ailments and irritations that can upset the best planned trip. Here we can help you and, perhaps, the doctor.

Some doctors will speak English well; others will know enough for your needs. But suppose there's something the doctor can't explain because of language difficulties? We've thought of that. As you'll see, this section has been arranged to enable you and the doctor to communicate. From pages 165 to 171, you find your part of the dialogue on the upper half of each page—the doctor's is on the lower half.

The whole section has been divided into three parts: illness, wounds, nervous tension. Page 171 is concerned with prescriptions and fees.

General

Can you get me a doctor?	**Bana bir doktor çağırır mısınız?**	bahnah beer doktor chahrır mıssınız
Is there a doctor here?	**Burada doktor var mı?**	boorahdah doktor vahr mı
Please telephone for a doctor immediately.	**Derhal bir doktora telefon edin, lüften.**	dehrhahl beer doktorah tehlehfon ehdeen lewtfehn
Where's there a doctor who speaks English?	**Nerede ingilizce bilen bir doktor vardır?**	nehrehdeh eeng'eeleezjeh beelehn beer doktor vahrdır
Is there an English/American hospital in town?	**Şehirde bir İngiliz/Amerikan hastanesi var mıdır?**	shehheerdeh beer eeng'eeleez/ ahmehreekahn hahstahnehssee vahr mıdır

DOCTOR

Where's the surgery (doctor's office)?	**Muayenehane nerededir?**	mooahyehnehhahneh nehrehdehdeer
What are the surgery (office) hours?	**Muayene saatleri kaçtan kaça kadar sürer?**	mooahyehneh sartlehree kahchtahn kahchah kahdahr sewrehr
Could the doctor come to see me here?	**Doktor beni muayene etmek için buraya gelebilir mi?**	doktor behnee mooahyehneh ehtmehk eecheen boorahyah gᵛehlehbeeleer mee
What time can the doctor come?	**Doktor ne zaman gelebilir?**	doktor neh zahmahn gᵛehlehbeeleer

Symptoms

Use this section to tell the doctor what's wrong. Basically, what he'll require to know is:

What? (ache, pain, bruise, etc.)
Where? (arm, stomach, etc.)
How long? (have you had the trouble)

Before you visit the doctor find out the answers to these questions by glancing through the pages that follow.

Parts of the body

ankle	**ayak bileği**	ahyahk beelehee
appendix	**apandis**	ahpahndeess
arm	**kol**	kol
artery	**atardamar**	ahtahrdahmahr
back	**sırt**	sırt
bladder	**idrar torbası**	eedrahr torbahssı
blood	**kan**	kahn
bone	**kemik**	kehmeek
breast	**göğüs**	gurewss
cheek	**yanak**	yahnahk
chest	**göğüs**	gurewss
shin	**çene**	chehneh
collar-bone	**köprücük kemiği**	kurprewjewk kehmeeee
ear	**kulak**	koolahk
elbow	**dirsek**	deersehk
eye	**göz**	gurz
face	**yüz**	yewz
finger	**parmak**	pahrmahk

foot	**ayak**	ahyahk
forehead	**alın**	ahlın
gland	**beze**	behzeh
hair	**saç**	sahch
hand	**el**	ehl
head	**baş**	bahsh
heart	**kalp**	kahlp
heel	**topuk**	topook
hip	**kalça**	kahlchah
intestines	**bağırsaklar**	bahrsahklahr
jaw	**çene kemiği**	chehneh kehmeeee
joint	**mafsal**	mahfsahl
kidney	**böbrek**	burbrehk
knee	**diz**	deez
knee cap	**diz kapağı**	deez kahpahı
leg	**bacak**	bahjahk
lip	**dudak**	doodahk
liver	**karaciğer**	kahrahjeeehr
lung	**akciğer**	ahkjeeehr
mouth	**ağız**	ahız
muscle	**adele**	ahdehleh
neck	**boyun**	boyoon
nerve	**sinir**	seeneer
nervous system	**sinir sistemi**	seeneer seestehmee
nose	**burun**	booroon
rib	**kaburga kemiği**	kahboorgah kehmeeee
shoulder	**omuz**	omooz
skin	**deri**	dehree
spine	**omurga**	omoorgah
stomach	**mide**	meedeh
tendon	**kiriş**	keereesh
thigh	**uyluk**	ooylook
throat	**boğaz**	boahz
thumb	**başparmak**	bahshpahrmahk
toe	**ayak parmağı**	ahyahk pahrmahı
tongue	**dil**	deel
tonsils	**bademcikler**	bahdehmjeeklehr
urine	**idrar**	eedrahr
vein	**toplar damar**	toplahr dahmahr
wrist	**bilek**	beelehk

DOCTOR

left/on the left side	right/on the right side
sol/sol tarafta	**sağ/sağ tarafta**
(sohl / sohl tahraf**tah**)	(sah / sah tahraf**tah**)

PATIENT

Part 1—Illness

I'm not feeling well.	Kendimi iyi hissetmiyorum.	kehndeemee eeyee heessehtmeeyoroom
I'm ill.	Hastayım.	hahstahyım
I've got a pain here.	Buramda bir ağrı var.	boorahmdah beer ahrı vahr
His/Her ... hurts.	...sı ağrıyor.	...sı ahrıyor
I've got (a)...		
headache	Başım ağrıyor.	bahshım ahrıyor
backache	Sırtım ağrıyor.	sırtım ahrıyor
fever	Ateşim var.	ahtehsheem vahr
sore throat	Boğazım ağrıyor.	boahzım ahrıyor
travel sickness	Yolculuk tutuyor.	yoljoolook tootooyor
I'm constipated.	Dışarı çıkamıyorum.	dıshahrı chıkahmıyoroom
I've been vomiting.	İstifra ettim.	eesteefrah ehtteem

DOCTOR

Kısım 1—Hastalık

Neyiniz var?	What's the trouble?
Nereniz ağrıyor?	Where does it hurt?
Bu ağrı sizi ne zamandan beri rahatsız ediyor?	How long have you had this pain?
Ne zamandan beri kendinizi böyle hissediyorsunuz?	How long have you been feeling like this?
Kolunuzu sıvayın, lütfen.	Roll up your sleeve.
Belinize kadar soyunun, lütfen.	Please undress down to the waist.
Pantolonunuzu ve külodunuzu çıkarın, lütfen.	Please remove your trousers and underpants.

PATIENT

I feel...

faint	Kendimi zayıf hissediyorum.	kehndeemee zahyıf heessehdeeyoroom
dizzy	Başım dönüyor.	bahshım durnewyor
nauseous	Bulantı var.	boolahnntı vahr
shivery	Titreme geliyor.	teetrehmeh gᵛehleeyor

I/He/She's got (a/an)...

abcess	Absesi var.	ahbsehssee vahr
asthma	Astımım var.	ahstımım vahr
boil	Çıbanım var.	chıbahnıhm var
chill	Üşüttüm.	ewshewttewm
cold	Nezleyim.	nehzlehyeem
constipation	Pekliğim var.	pehkleeyeem vahr
convulsions	İntilaç içindeyim.	eenteelahch eecheendehyeem
cramps	Kramp giriyor.	krahmp gᵛeereeyor
diarrhoea	Diyare oldum.	deeyahreh oldoom
fever	Ateşim var.	ahtehsheem vahr
haemorrhoids	Bâsurum var.	barssooroom vahr

DOCTOR

Buraya uzanın, lütfen.	Please lie down over here.
Ağzınızı açın.	Open your mouth.
Derin nefes alın.	Breathe deeply.
Öksürün, lütfen.	Cough, please.
Ateşinizi ölçeceğim.	I'll take your temperature.
Tansiyonunuzu ölçeceğim.	I'm going to take your blood pressure.
Bu ilk defa mı başınıza geliyor?	Is this the first time you've had this?
Size bir iğne yapacağım.	I'll give you an injection.
İdrar/Kazurat numunesi istiyorum.	I want a sample of your urine/stools.

DOCTOR

PATIENT

hay fever	Saman nezlesi oldum.	sahmahn nehzlehssee oldoom
hernia	Fıtığım var.	fıtıım vahr
indigestion	Hazımsızlık çekiyorum.	hahzımsızlık chehkeeyoroom
inflammation of...	...mda iltihap var.	...mdah eelteehahp vahr
influenza	Grip oldum.	greep oldoom
morning sickness	Bulantı oluyor.	boolahntı olooyor
rheumatism	Romatizmam var.	romahteezmahm vahr
stiff neck	Boynum tutuldu.	boynoom tootooldoo
sunburn	Güneşte çok yandım.	gʸewnehshteh chok yahndım
sunstroke	Güneş çarptı.	gʸewnehsh chahrptı
tonsillitis	Anjin oldum.	ahnzheen oldoom
ulcer	Ülserim var.	ewlsehreem vahr
whooping cough	Boğmaca oldum.	bomahjah oldoom
It's nothing serious, I hope?	Ümit ederim ki ciddî birşey yoktur.	ewmeet ehdehreem kee jeeddee beershay yoktoor
I'd like you to prescribe some medicine for me.	Bana birkaç ilâç yazmanızı rica edeceğim.	bahnah beerkahch eelarch yahzmahnızı reejah ehdehjeheem

DOCTOR

Merak edecek birşey yok.	It's nothing to worry about.
... gün yatakta kalmanız lâzım.	You must stay in bed for ...days.
	You've got...
Apandisitiniz var.	an appendicitis
Gripsiniz.	influenza
... iltihaplanması var.	an inflammation of...
Mafsal iltihabı var.	arthritis
Nezlesiniz.	a cold
Yemekten zehirlenmişsiniz.	food poisoning
Zatürresiniz.	pneumonia
Genel çek-ap için hastahaneye gitmenizi uygun görüyorum.	I want you to go to the hospital for a general check-up.
Size bir antibiyotik yazacağım.	I'll prescribe an antibiotic.

DOCTOR

PATIENT

I'm a diabetic.	Şeker hastasıyım.	shehkehr hahstahssıyım
I've a cardiac condition.	Kalp hastasıyım.	kahlp hahstahssıyım
I had a heart attack in...	... enfarktüs geçirdim.	... ehnfahrktewss gᵛehcheerdeem
I'm allergic to...	...ya alerjim var.	...yah ahlehrzheem vahr
This is my usual medicine.	Genellikle bu ilâcı alırım.	gᵛehnehlleekleh boo eelarjı ahlırım
I need this medicine.	Bu ilâca ihtiyacım var.	boo eelarjah eehteeyahjım vahr
I'm expecting a baby.	Bebek bekliyorum.	behbehk behkleeyoroom
Can I travel?	Seyahat edebilir miyim?	sehyahhaht ehdehbeeleer meeyeem

DOCTOR

Ensülin dozunuz nedir?	What dose of insulin are you taking?
Enjeksiyonla mı, yoksa ağız yolu ile mi?	Injection or oral?
Bundan evvel nasıl bir tedavi gördünüz?	What treatment have you been having?
Daha önce hangi ilaçları aldınız?	What medicine have you been taking?
Önemsiz bir kriz geçirmişsiniz.	You've had a slight heart attack.
Türkiye'de ... kullanmıyoruz. Bu ona çok benzer.	We don't use ... in Turkey. This is very similar.
Bebeği ne zaman bekliyorsunuz?	When's the baby due?
...ya kadar seyahat etmemelisiniz.	You can't travel until...

PATIENT

Part 2—Wounds

Could you have a look at this...?	Şu ... muayene eder misiniz?	shoo ... mooahyehneh ehdehr meesseeneez
blister	su toplamasını	soo toplahmahssını
boil	çıbanı	chıbahnı
bruise	çürüğü	chewrewew
burn	yanığı	yahnıı
cut	kesiği	kehsseeee
graze	sıyrığı	sıyrıı
insect bite	böcek ısırığını	burjehk ıssırını
lump	şişi	sheeshee
rash	indifayı/sivilceleri	eendeefahyı/seeveel-jehlehree
sting	iğne yarasını	eeneh yahrahssını
swelling	şişliği	sheeshleeee
wound	yarayı	yahrahyı
I can't move my...	... mı oynatamıyorum.	...mı oynahtahmıyoroom
It hurts.	Acıyor.	ahjıyor

DOCTOR

Kısım 2—Aralar

Mikrop kapmış (kapmamış).	It's (not) infected.
Disk kayması var.	You've got a slipped disc.
Röntgeninizin çekilmesi lâzım.	I want you to have an X-ray.
	It's...
Kırılmış/Burkulmuş. Çıkmış./Yırtılmış.	broken/sprained dislocated/torn
Bir adeleniz ezilmiş.	You've pulled a muscle.
Size bir antiseptik veriyorum.	I'll give you an antiseptic.
Önemli değil.	It's not serious.
... gün sonra gelip beni görmeniz lâzım.	I want you to come and see me in...day's time.

PATIENT

Part 3—Nervous tension

I'm in a nervous state.	**Sinirlerim bozuk.**	seeneerlehreem bozook
I'm feeling depressed.	**Kendimi bitkin hissediyorum.**	kehndeemee beetkeen heessehdeeyoroom
I want some sleeping pills.	**Uyku hapı istiyorum.**	ooykoo hahpı eesteeyoroom
I can't eat.	**Yiyemiyorum.**	yeeyehmeeyoroom
I can't sleep.	**Uyuyamiyorum.**	ooyooyahmıyoroom
I'm having nightmares.	**Kâbus görüyorum.**	karbooss gurrewyoroom
Can you prescribe a...?	**Bir ... yazar mısınız?**	beer ... yahzahr mıssınız
anti-depressant	**münnebih**	mewnehbeehh
sedative	**müsekkin**	mewsehkkeen
tranquillizer	**trankilizan**	trahnkeeleeezahn

DOCTOR

Kısım 3—Sinir bozukluğu

Sinirleriniz gergin.	You're suffering from nervous tension.
Dinlenmeye ihtiyacınız var.	You need a rest.
Daha önce hangi haplardan aldınız?	What pills have you been taking?
Günde kaç tane?	How many a day?
Kendinizi ne zamandan beri böyle hissediyorsunuz?	How long have you been feeling like this?
Size birkaç hap yazacağım.	I'll prescribe some pills.
Size bir müsekkin/münnebih vereceğim.	I'll give you a sedative/anti-depressant.

DOCTOR

PATIENT

Prescriptions and dosage

What kind of medicine is this?	**Bu ne tür bir ilâçtır?**	boo neh tewr beer eelarchtır
How many times a day should I take it?	**Bundan günde kaç defa almalıyım?**	boondahn gᵛewndeh kahch dehfah ahlmahlıyım
Must I swallow them whole?	**Bunları bütün olarak mı yutacağım?**	boonlahrı bewtewn olahrahk mı yootahjahım

Fee

How much do I owe you?	**Borcum ne kadar?**	borjoom neh kahdahr
Do I pay you now or will you send me your bill?	**Şimdi mi ödeyeyim yoksa bana faturayı mı göndereceksiniz?**	sheemdee mee urdehyehyeem yoksah bahnah fahtoorahyı mı gurndehrehjehkseeneez
Thanks for your help, Doctor.	**Yardımınıza teşekkürler, Doktor.**	yahrdımınızah tehshehkkewrlehr doktor

DOCTOR

DOCTOR

Reçete ve dozaj

Bu ilâçtan her ... saat ... çay kaşığı alın.	Take ... teaspoons of this medicine every ... hours.
... bir bardak su ile 2 hapı alın.	Take 2 pills with a glass of water...
Günde ... defa	... times a day
Her yemekten önce	before each meal
Her yemekten sonra	after each meal
Sabahları	in the mornings
Gece	at night

Ücret

100 Lira, lütfen.	That's 100 liras, please.
Lütfen şimdi ödeyin.	Please pay me now.
Size fatura yollayacağım.	I'll send you a bill.

FOR NUMBERS, see page 175

Dentist

Can you recommend a good dentist?	İyi bir dişçi tavsiye edebilir misiniz?	eeyee beer deeshchee tahvseeyeh ehdehbeeleer meesseeneez
Can I make an (urgent) appointment to see Doctor...?	Doktor ...den (acele) randevu alabilir miyim?	doktor ...dehn (ahjehleh) rahndehvoo ahlahbeeleer meeyeem
Can't you possibly make it earlier than that?	Daha erkene almanıza imkân yok mu?	dahhah ehrkehneh ahlmahnızah eemkarn yok moo
I've a toothache.	Dişim ağrıyor.	deesheem ahrıyor
I've an abcess.	Dişimde abse var.	deesheemdeh ahbseh vahr
This tooth hurts.	Bu dişim ağrıyor.	boo deesheem ahrıyor
at the top	yukarıda	yookarıdah
at the bottom	aşağıda	ahshahdah
in the front	önde	urndeh
at the back	arkada	ahrkahdah
Can you fix it temporarily?	Şimdilik bir çaresine bakabilir misiniz?	sheemdeeleek beer chahrehseeneh bahkahbeeleer meesseeneez
I don't want it extracted.	Çekilmesini istemiyorum.	chehkeelmehsseenee eestehmeeyoroom
I've lost a filling.	Dolgumu düşürdüm.	dolgoomoo dewshewrdewm
The gum is...	Diş etlerim...	deesh ehtlehreem...
very sore	çok ağrıyor	chok ahrıyor
bleeding	kanıyor	kahnıyohr

Dentures

I've broken this denture.	Takma dişim kırıldı.	tahkmah deesheem kırıldı
Can you repair this denture?	Bu takma dişi tamir edebilir misiniz?	boo tahkmah deeshee tahmeer ehdehbeeleer meesseeneez
When will it be ready?	Ne zaman hazır olur?	neh zahmahn hahzır oloor

Optician

I've broken my glasses.	**Gözlüğümü kırdım.**	gurzlewmew kırdım
Can you repair them for me?	**Tamir edebilir misiniz?**	tahmeer ehdehbeeleer meesseeneez
When will they be ready?	**Ne zaman hazır olur?**	neh zahmahn hahzır oloor
Can you change the lenses?	**Camları değiştire-bilir misiniz?**	jahmlahrı deheeshteereh-beeleer meesseeneez
I want tinted lenses.	**Renkli cam istiyorum.**	rehnklee jahm eesteeyoroom
I want some contact lenses.	**Kontakt lens istiyorum.**	kontahkt lehnss eesteeyoroom
I'd like to buy a pair of binoculars.	**Dürbün almak istiyorum.**	dewrbewn ahlmahk eesteeyoroom
I'd like to buy a pair of sun-glasses.	**Guneş gözlüğü almak istiyorum.**	gʸewnehsh gurzlewew ahlmahk eesteeyoroom
How much do I owe you?	**Borcum ne kadar?**	borjoom neh kahdahr
Do I pay you now or will you send me your bill?	**Şimdi mi ödeyeyim, yoksa bana fatura mı göndereceksiniz?**	sheemdee mee urdehyehyeem yoksah bahnah fahtoorah mı gurndehrehjehkseneez

Reference section

Where do you come from?

Africa	**Afrika**	ahfreekah
Asia	**Asya**	ahssyah
Australia	**Avustralya**	ahvoostrahlyah
Bulgaria	**Bulgaristan**	boolgvahreestahn
Canada	**Kanada**	kahnahdah
China	**Çin**	cheen
Cyprus	**Kıbrıs**	kıbrıss
Egypt	**Mısır**	mıssır
England	**İngiltere**	eengveeltehreh
Europe	**Avrupa**	ahvroopah
France	**Fransa**	frahnsah
Germany	**Almanya**	ahlmahnyah
Great Britain	**Büyük Britanya**	bewyewk breetahnyah
Greece	**Yunanistan**	yoonahneestahn
Iraq	**Irak**	ırahk
Iran	**İran**	eerahn
Ireland	**İrlanda**	eerlahndah
Israel	**İsrail**	eesraheel
Italy	**İtalya**	eetahlyah
Japan	**Japonya**	zhahpohnyah
Jordan	**Ürdün**	ewrdewn
Lebanon	**Lübnan**	lewbnahn
Middle East	**Orta Doğu**	ortah dooo
New Zealand	**Yeni Zelanda**	yehnee zehlahndah
North America	**Kuzey Amerika**	koozay ahmehreekah
Saudi Arabia	**Suudî Arabistan**	soodee ahrahbeestahn
Scandinavia	**İskandinavya**	eeskahndeenahvyah
Scotland	**İskoçya**	eeskochyah
South Africa	**Güney Afrika**	gvewnay ahfreekah
South America	**Güney Amerika**	gvewnay ahmehreekah
Spain	**İspanya**	eespahnyah
Switzerland	**İsviçre**	eesveechreh
Syria	**Suriye**	sooreeyeh
Turkey	**Türkiye**	tewrkeeyeh
USA	**Amerika Birleşik Devletleri**	ahmehreekah beerlehsheek dehvlehtlehree
USSR	**Sovyetler Birliği**	sovyehtlehr beerleeee
Wales	**Galler Ülkesi**	gahllehr ewlkehssee

Numbers

1	bir	beer
2	iki	eekee
3	üç	ewch
4	dört	durrt
5	beş	behsh
6	altı	ahltı
7	yedi	yehdee
8	sekiz	sehkeez
9	dokuz	dokooz
10	on	on
11	on bir	on beer
12	on iki	on eekee
13	on üç	on ewch
14	on dört	on durrt
15	on beş	on behsh
16	on altı	on ahltı
17	on yedi	on yehdee
18	on sekiz	on sehkeez
19	on dokuz	on dokooz
20	yirmi	yeermee
21	yirmi bir	yeermee beer
22	yirmi iki	yeermee eekee
23	yirmi üç	yeermee ewch
24	yirmi dört	yeermee durrt
25	yirmi beş	yeermee behsh
26	yirmi altı	yeermee ahltı
27	yirmi yedi	yeermee yehdee
28	yirmi sekiz	yeermee sehkeez
29	yirmi dokuz	yeermee dokooz
30	otuz	otooz
31	otuz bir	otooz beer
32	otuz iki	otooz eekee
33	otuz üç	otooz ewch
40	kırk	kırk
41	kırk bir	kirk beer
42	kırk iki	kırk eekee
43	kırk üç	kirk ewch
50	elli	ehllee
51	elli bir	ehllee beer
52	elli iki	ehllee eekee
53	elli üç	ehllee ewch
60	altmış	ahltmısh
61	altmış bir	ahltmısh beer
62	altmış iki	ahltmısh eekee

63	altmış üç	ahltmısh ewch
70	yetmiş	yehtmeesh
71	yetmiş bir	yehtmeesh beer
72	yetmiş iki	yehtmeesh eekee
73	yetmiş üç	yehtmeesh ewch
80	seksen	sehksehn
81	seksen bir	sehksehn beer
82	seksen iki	sehksehn eekee
83	seksen üç	sehksehn ewch
90	doksan	doksahn
91	doksan bir	doksahn beer
92	doksan iki	doksahn eekee
93	doksan üç	doksahn ewch
100	yüz	yewz
101	yüz bir	yewz beer
102	yüz iki	yewz eekee
110	yüz on	yewz on
120	yüz yirmi	yewz yeermee
130	yüz otuz	yewz otooz
140	yüz kırk	yewz kırk
150	yüz elli	yewz ehllee
160	yüz altmış	yewz ahltmısh
170	yüz yetmiş	yewz yehtmeesh
180	yüz seksen	yewz sehksehn
190	yüz doksan	yewz doksahn
200	iki yüz	eekee yewz
300	üç yüz	ewch yewz
400	dört yüz	durrt yewz
500	beş yüz	behsh yewz
600	altı yüz	ahltı yewz
700	yedi yüz	yehdee yewz
800	sekiz yüz	sehkeez yewz
900	dokuz yüz	dokooz yewz
1000	bin	been
1100	bin yüz	been yewz
1200	bin iki yüz	been eekee yewz
2000	iki bin	eekee been
5000	beş bin	behsh been
10,000	on bin	on been
50,000	elli bin	ehllee been
100,000	yüz bin	yewz been
1,000,000	bir milyon	beer meelyon
1,000,000,000	bir milyar	beer meelyahr

first	birinci	beereenjee
second	ikinci	eekeenjee
third	üçüncü	ewchewnjew
fourth	dördüncü	durrdewnjew
fifth	beşinci	behsheenjee
sixth	altıncı	ahltınjı
seventh	yedinci	yehdeenjee
eighth	sekizinci	sehkeezeenjee
ninth	dokuzuncu	dokoozoonjoo
tenth	onuncu	onoonjoo
once	bir kere	beer kehreh
twice	iki kere	eekee kehreh
three times	üç kere	ewch kehreh
half	yarım	yahrım
a quarter	dörtte bir	durrtteh beer
one third	üçte bir	ewchteh beer
a pair of	bir çift	beer cheeft
a dozen	bir düzine	beer dewzeeneh
1982	bin dokuz yüz seksen iki	been dokooz yewz sehksehn eekee
1983	bin dokuz yüz seksen üç	been dokooz yewz sehksehn ewch
1984	bin dokuz yüz seksen dört	been dokooz yewz sehksehn durrt

Time

**on-ikiyi çeyrek
geçiyor**
(ohn-eekee**yee** chay**rehk**
g**v**ehchee**yor**)

biri yirmi geçiyor
(bee**ree** yeer**mee**
g**v**ehchee**yor**)

**ikiyi yirmi-beş
geçiyor**
(eekee**yee** yeer**mee**-beh**sh**
g**v**ehchee**yor**)

üç buçuk
(ewch boo**chook**)

beşe yirmi-beş var
(beh**sheh** yeer**mee**-beh**sh**
vahr)

altıya yirmi var
(ahl**tı**yah yeer**mee** vahr)

yediye çeyrek var
(yeh**dee**yeh chay**rehk**
vahr)

sekize on var
(seh**kee**zeh ohn vahr)

dokuza beş var
(doh**koo**zah behsh vahr)

saat on
(sart ohn)

on-biri beş geçiyor
(ohn-bee**ree** behsh
g**v**ehchee**yor**)

on-ikiyi on geçiyor
(ohn-eekee**yee** ohn
g**v**ehchee**yor**)

Useful expressions

What time is it?	Saat kaç?	sart kahch
It's...	Saat...	sart
Excuse me. Can you tell me the time?	Affedersiniz, saa-tiniz kaç, acaba?	ahffehdehrseeneez sartınız kahch ahjahbah
I'll meet you at... tomorrow.	Yarın saat ...'de/da sizinle buluşacağım.	yahrın sart...deh/dah seezeenleh boolooshahjarm
I'm sorry I'm late.	Özür dilerim, geç kaldım.	urzewr deelehreem gᵛehch kahldım
At what time does... open?	... saat kaçta açılır?	...sart kahchtah ahchılır
At what time does... close?	... saat kaçta kapanır?	...sart kahchtah kahpahnır
How long will it last?	Ne kadar sürer?	neh kahdahr sewrehr
What time will it end?	Saat kaçta biter?	sart kahchtah beetehr
At what time should I be there?	Saat kaçta orada olayım?	sart kahchtah orahdah olahyım
At what time will you be there?	Siz saat kaçta orada olacaksınız?	seez sart kahchtah orahdah olahjahksınız
Can I come...?	Saat ... gelebilirmiyim?	sart... gᵛehlehbeeleermeeyeem
at 8 o'clock/at 2:30	sekizde/iki buçukta	sehkeezdeh/eekee boochooktah
after/afterwards	sonra	sonrah
before/beforehand	önce	urnjeh
early	erken	ehrkehn
in time	saatinde	sarteendeh
late	geç	gᵛech
midnight	gece yarısı	gᵛehjeh yahrıssı
noon	öğleyin	urlehyeen
hour	saat	sart
minute	dakika	dahkeekah
second	saniye	sahneeyeh
quarter of an hour	çeyrek saat	chayrehk sart
half an hour	yarım saat	yahrım sart

REFERENCE SECTION

Alaska Time
Pacific Time
Mountain Time
Central Time
Eastern Time
Atlantic Time

Western European Time (G.M.T.)
Central European Time
Eastern European Time

Date Line

| 1 a.m. | 2 a.m. | 3 a.m. | 4 a.m. | 5 a.m. | 6 a.m. | 7 a.m. | 8 a.m. | 9 a.m. | 10 a.m. | 11 a.m. | noon | 1 p.m. | 2 p.m. | 3 p.m. | 4 p.m. | 5 p.m. | 6 p.m. | 7 p.m. | 8 p.m. | 9 p.m. | 10 p.m. | 11 p.m. | mid-night |

Countries which have adopted a time differing from that in the corresponding time zone. Note that also in the U.S.S.R. official time is one hour ahead of the time in each corresponding time zone. In summer,

Days

What day is it today?	**Bugün günlerden ne?**	boog^yewn g^yewnlehrdehn neh
Sunday	**Pazar**	pahzahr
Monday	**Pazartesi**	pahzahrtehssee
Tuesday	**Salı**	sahlı
Wednesday	**Çarşamba**	chahrshahmbah
Thursday	**Perşembe**	pehrshehmbeh
Friday	**Cuma**	joomah
Saturday	**Cumartesi**	joomahrtehssee
in the morning	**sabahleyin**	sahbahhlehyeen
during the day	**gün esnasında**	g^yewn ehsnahssındah
in the afternoon	**öğleden sonra**	urlehdehn sonrah
in the evening	**akşam**	ahkshahm
at night	**geceleyin**	g^yehjehlehyeen
the day before yesterday	**evvelki gün**	ehvvehlkee g^yewn
	dün	dewn
today	**bugün**	boog^yewn
tomorrow	**yarın**	yahrın
the day after tomorrow	**öbür gün**	urbewr g^yewn
	bir önceki gün	beer urnjehkee g^yewn
the day before	**ertesi gün**	ehrtehssee g^yewn
the next day	**iki gün önce**	eekee g^yewn urnjeh
two days ago	**üç gün sonra**	ewch g^yewn sonrah
in three days' time	**geçen hafta**	g^yehchehn hahftah
last week	**gelecek hafta**	g^yehlehjehk hahftah
for two weeks	**on beş günlüğüne**	on behsh g^yewnlewneh
birthday	**doğum günü**	dooom g^yewnew
day	**gün**	g^yewn
day off	**tatil günü**	tahteel g^yewnew
holidays	**tatil**	tahteel
month	**ay**	ahy
school holidays	**yaz tatili**	yahz tahteelee
vacation	**tatil**	tahteel
week	**hafta**	hahftah
weekday	**âdi gün**	ardee g^yewn
weekend	**hafta sonu**	hahftah sonoo
working day	**iş günü**	eesh g^yewnew

Months

January	**Ocak**	ojahk
February	**Şubat**	shoo**baht**
March	**Mart**	mahrt
April	**Nisan**	nee**ssahn**
May	**Mayıs**	mahyıs
June	**Haziran**	hahzeerahn
July	**Temmuz**	tehm**mooz**
August	**Ağustos**	ahoostoss
September	**Eylül**	ay**lewl**
October	**Ekim**	eh**keem**
November	**Kasım**	kahsım
December	**Aralık**	ahrah**lık**
since June	**Hazirandan beri**	hahzeerahn**dahn** behree
during the month of August	**Ağustos ayı boyunca**	ahoostoss ahyı boyoonjah
last month	**geçen ay**	gᵉehchehn ahy
next month	**gelecek ay**	gᵉehlehjehk ahy
the month before	**önceki ay**	urnjehkee ahy
the following month	**ondan sonraki ay**	ondahn sonrah**kee** ahy
July 1	**1 Temmuz**	1 tehm**mooz**
March 17	**17 Mart**	17 mahrt

Letter headings are written thus:

Ankara, August 17, 19.. **Ankara, 17 Ağustos, 19..**

Istanbul, July 1, 19.. **Istanbul, 1 Haziran, 19..**

Seasons

spring	**ilkbahar**	eelkbah**hahr**
summer	**yaz**	yahz
autumn	**sonbahar**	sonbah**hahr**
winter	**kış**	kısh
in spring	**ilkbaharda**	eelkbah**hahr**dah
during the summer	**yaz boyunca**	yahz boyoonjah
in autumn	**sonbaharda**	sonbah**hahr**dah
during the winter	**kış boyunca**	kısh boyoonjah

Public holidays

These are the public holidays when banks, schools, offices and shops are closed:

January 1	New Year's Day	**Yılbaşı**
April 23	National Sovereignty and Children's Day	**23 Nisan Çocuk Bayramı**
May 1	Spring Holiday	**Bahar Bayramı**
May 19	Youth Day	**Gençlik ve Spor Bayramı**
May 27	Freedom and Constitution Day	**Hürriyet ve Devrim Bayramı**
August 30	Victory Day	**Zafer Bayramı**
October 29	Republic Day	**Cumhuriyet Bayramı**

Aside from the above civic holidays, there are two important Moslem holy periods. The first of these is called *şeker bayramı* (sugar holy days) and lasts three days. It follows four weeks of fasting during the Islamic month of Ramadan. Three months after that comes the four-day *kurban bayramı* (holy days of sacrifice). Each year these holy periods fall ten days later than the previous year.

The year-round temperatures

	Ankara	Istanbul	Izmir
January	32 °F	41 °F	46 °F
February	32	41	48
March	41	44	51
April	51	51	59
May	60	60	68
June	68	68	75
July	73	73	80
August	73	73	80
September	64	66	73
October	53	50	64
November	44	53	57
December	35	46	50

Common abbreviations

A.A.	Anadolu Ajansı	a Turkish press agency
A.B.D.	Amerika Birleşik Devletleri	U.S.A.
Apt.	apartman	apartment
As.	Askerî/asistan	military/assistant
As. İz.	Askerî İnzibat	military police
B.	Bay	Mr.
B.M.	Birleşmiş Milletler	United Nations
B.M.M.	Büyük Millet Meclisi	Turkish National Assembly (House of Deputies)
Bn.	Bayan	Mrs., Miss
Cad.	cadde	avenue
D.D.Y.	Devlet Deniz Yolları	Turkish National Shipping Lines
Doç.	doçent	professor
Gnl.	general	general
İ.E.T.T.	İstanbul Elektrik Tramvay Tünel	Istanbul Municipal Transport
İst.	İstanbul	İstanbul
Koll. Şti.	kollektif şirketi	Ltd. (Inc.)
Krş	kuruş	kurus (see currency)
Mah.	Mahallesi	borough, quarter of the city
M.Ö.	Milâttan Önce	B.C.
M.S.	Milâttan Sonra	A.D.
Ord. Prof.	ordinaryüs profesör	professor
P.K.	posta kutusu	post office box
P.T.T.	Posta Telegraf Telefon	Post, Telegraph and Telephone Office
Sok.	sokak	street
S.S.C.B.	Sovjet Sosyalist Cumhuriyetler Birliği	U.S.S.R.
T.B.M.M.	Türkiye Büyük Millet Meclisi	Parliament of Turkey
T.C.	Türkiye Cumhuriyeti	Republic of Turkey
T.C.D.D.Y.	Türkiye Cumhuriyeti Devlet Demir Yolları	Turkish State Railways
T.L.	Türk Lirası	Turkish Liras
T.T.O.K.	Türk Turing Otomobil Kurumu	Turkish Touring Club
Tel.	telefon	telephone
T.H.Y.	Türk Hava Yolları	Turkish Airlines
T.R.T.	Türkiye Radyo ve Televizyonu	Turkish Radio and Television Company

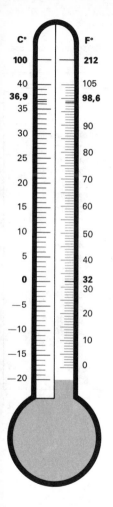

Conversion tables

Centimetres and inches

To change centimetres into inches, multiply by .39.

To change inches into centimetres, multiply by 2.54.

	in.	feet	yards
1 mm	0,039	0,003	0,001
1 cm	0,39	0,03	0,01
1 dm	3,94	0,32	0,10
1 m	39,40	3,28	1,09

	mm	cm	m
1 in.	25,4	2,54	0,025
1 ft.	304,8	30,48	0,304
1 yd.	914,4	91,44	0,914

(32 metres = 35 yards)

Temperature

To convert Centigrade into degrees Fahrenheit, multiply Centigrade by 1.8 and add 32.

To convert degrees Fahrenheit into Centigrade, subtract 32 from Fahrenheit and divide by 1.8.

Metres and feet

The figure in the middle stands for both metres and feet, e.g.,
1 metre = 3.281 ft. and 1 foot = 0.30 m.

Metres		Feet
0.30	1	3.281
0.61	2	6.563
0.91	3	9.843
1.22	4	13.124
1.52	5	16.403
1.83	6	19.686
2.13	7	22.967
2.44	8	26.248
2.74	9	29.529
3.05	10	32.810
3.35	11	36.091
3.66	12	39.372
3.96	13	42.635
4.27	14	45.934
4.57	15	49.215
4.88	16	52.496
5.18	17	55.777
5.49	18	59.058
5.79	19	62.339
6.10	20	65.620
7.62	25	82.023
15.24	50	164.046
22.86	75	246.069
30.48	100	328.092

Other conversion charts

REFERENCE SECTION

Weight conversion

The figure in the middle stands for both kilograms and pounds,
e.g., 1 kilogram = 2.205 lb. and 1 pound = 0.45 kilograms.

Kilograms (kg.)		Avoirdupois pounds
0.45	1	2.205
0.90	2	4.405
1.35	3	6.614
1.80	4	8.818
2.25	5	11.023
2.70	6	13.227
3.15	7	15.432
3.60	8	17.636
4.05	9	19.840
4.50	10	22.045
6.75	15	33.068
9.00	20	44.889
11.25	25	55.113
22.50	50	110.225
33.75	75	165.338
45.00	100	220.450

NORTH
KUZEY
koo**zeh**y

WEST
BATI
bahtı

EAST
DOĞU
dooo

SOUTH
GÜNEY
gewnehy

REFERENCE SECTION

What does that sign mean?

You're sure to encounter some of these signs or notices on your trip:

Açık	Open
Asansör	Lift (elevator)
Bayanlar	Ladies
Baylar	Gentlemen
Bisiklet yolu	Cycle path
Boş	Vacant
Boş yer yok/Boş oda yok	No vacancy/No rooms
Çekiniz	Pull
Çıkış	Exit
Danışma	Information
Dikkat	Caution
Dikkat, köpek var!	Beware of the dog
Dokunmayınız	Do not touch
Dolu/doludur	Sold out
Giriş	Entrance
Giriş serbesttir	Entrance free
Girmek yasaktır	No entrance/No admission
İçilmez	Do not drink
İçme suyu	Drinking water
İmdat çıkışı	Emergency exit
İtiniz	Push
Kapalı	Closed
Kapıyı çalmadan giriniz	Enter without knocking
Kılavuz	Guide
Kiralık	To let/For hire (rent)
Lütfen zili çalınız	Please ring
Meşgûl	Occupied
Ölüm tehlikesi	Danger of death
Özel	Private
Satılık	For sale
Sıcak	Hot
Sigara içilmez	No smoking
Soğuk	Cold
Tehlike	Danger
Tenzilâtlı satışlar	Sales
Tercüman	Interpreter
Tutulmuş	Reserved
Vezne	Cashier's
Yasakbölge	Trespassers will be prosecuted
... yasaktır	... forbidden
Yer kalmamıştır	Sold out

Emergency!

By the time the emergency is upon you it's too late to turn to this page to find the Turkish for "I'll scream if you...". So have a look at this short list beforehand—and, if you want to be on the safe side, learn the expressions shown in capitals.

Be quick	**Acele edin**	ahjehleh ehdeen
Call the police	**Polis çağırın**	polees chahrın
CAREFUL	**DİKKAT**	deekkaht
Come here	**Buraya gelin**	boorahyah gᵛehleen
Come in	**Girin**	gᵛeereen
Danger	**Tehlike**	tehhleekeh
Fire	**Ateş**	ahtehsh
Gas	**Gaz**	gahz
Get a doctor	**Doktor çağırın**	doktor chahrın
HELP	**YARDIM EDİN**	yahrdım ehdeen
Get help quickly	**Çabuk imdat isteyin**	chahbook eemdaht eestehyeen
I'm ill	**Hastayım**	hahstahyım
I'm lost	**Kayboldum**	kahyboldoom
I've lost my...	**...ımı kaybettim**	...ımı kahybehtteem
Keep your hands to yourself	**Çekin ellerinizi**	chehkeen ehllehreeneezee
Leave me alone	**Beni rahat bırakın**	behnee rahhaht bırahkın
Lie down	**Yatın**	yahtın
Listen	**Dinleyin**	deenlehyeen
Listen to me	**Beni dinleyin**	behnee deenlehyeen
LOOK	**BAKIN**	bahkın
Look out	**Dikkat**	deekkaht
POLICE	**POLİS**	poleess
Quick	**Çabuk**	chahbook
STOP	**DUR**	door
Stop here	**Burada durun**	boorahdah dooroon
Stop that man	**Şu adamı durdurun**	shoo ahdahmı doordooroon
Stop thief	**Hırsızı yakalayın**	hırsızı yahkahlahyın
Stop or I'll scream	**Durun, yoksa bağırım**	dooroon yoksah bahrırım

FOR CAR ACCIDENTS, see page 149

REFERENCE SECTION

Index

Quick reference page

Here are some of the phrases and expressions you'll probably need most frequently on your trip.

Please.	**Lütfen.**	lewtfehn
Thank you.	**Teşekkür ederim.**	tehshehkkewr ehdehreem
Yes/No.	**Evet/Hayır.**	ehveht/hahyır
Excuse me.	**Affedersiniz.**	ahffehdehrseeneez
Waiter, please.	**Garson, lütfen.**	gahrson lewtfehn
How much is that?	**Bu kaçadır.**	boo kahchahdır
Where are the toilets?	**Tuvaletler nerede?**	toovahlehtlehr nehrehdeh

OO	Toilets
Baylar (bahylahr)	**Bayanlar** (bahyahnlar)

Could you tell me...?	**... olduğunu söyleyebilir misiniz?**	...oldoonoo surlehyeh-beeleer meesseeneez
where/when/why	**Nerede/Ne zaman/Niçin**	nehrehdeh/neh zahmahn/neecheen
Help me, please.	**Lütfen bana yardım edin.**	lewtfehn bahnah yahrdım ehdeen
What time is it?	**Saat kaç?**	sart kahch
one/first two/second three/third	**bir/birinci iki/ikinci üç/üçüncü**	beer/beereenjee eekee/eekeenjee ewch/ewchewnjew
What does this mean? I don't understand.	**Bu ne demek? Anlamıyorum.**	boo neh dehmehk? ahnlahmıyoroom
Do you speak English?	**İngilizce biliyor musunuz?**	eengveeleezjeh beeleeyor moossoonooz